The
50 GREATEST PUBS
in
Central London

A Thirsty Tours® Publication

Ian Hirst

Michael Terence Publishing

First published in paperback by
Michael Terence Publishing in 2019
www.mtp.agency

Copyright © 2019 Ian Hirst

Ian Hirst has asserted the right to be identified as the
author of this work in accordance with the
Copyright, Designs and Patents Act 1988

ISBN 9781913289539

No part of this publication may be reproduced, stored in a retrieval system,
or transmitted, in any form or by any means, electronic, mechanical,
photocopying, recording or otherwise,
without the prior permission of the publishers

Photography by Mike Feather
www.mikefeather.com

Central London Pub Map
Copyright © DesignCrowd

Cover design
Copyright © 2019 Michael Terence Publishing

Contents

Foreword i
   Introduction and Background i
   The Public House and Associated Definitions i
   Definitions of Central London iii
   London Underground - The Circle Line iii
   Approach to the Selection of the 50 Greatest Pubs iii

The 50 Greatest Pubs in Central London 1
   The Argyll 4
   Black Friar 6
   The Cambridge 8
   Centre Page 10
   Churchill Arms 12
   Cittie of Yorke 14
   Cockpit 16
   Comptons 18
   Cross Keys 20
   Duke of Argyll 22
   East India Arms 24
   Fitzroy Tavern 26
   The Footman 28
   French House 30
   The Grenadier 32
   The Guinea 34
   Hand & Shears 36
   Hoop & Grapes 38
   The Hope 40
   Jamaica Wine House 42
   Lamb & Flag 44

Lamb Tavern	46
Lord Aberconway	48
Lord Raglan	50
Nags Head	52
Nell Gwynne	54
Old Bank of England	56
Old Bell	58
Old Doctor Butlers Head	60
Old Red Lion	62
Princess Louise	64
Punch Tavern	66
Queen's Larder	68
Red Lion	70
Red Lion	72
The Salisbury	74
Sherlock Holmes	76
Ship & Shovell	78
Ship Tavern	80
Star Tavern	82
The Swan	84
Two Brewers	86
Viaduct Tavern	88
Waxy O'Connors	90
White Hart	92
Williamson's Tavern	94
Ye Olde Cheshire Cheese	96
Ye Olde Cock Tavern	98
Ye Olde Mitre	100
Ye Olde Watling	102
Honourable Mentions	105
Coach & Horses	106

Hoop & Grapes	107
Sun in Splendour	108
Index	109
Author's Acknowledgements	115

Foreword

Introduction and Background

There have been many books published about London pubs, although with some subjectivity applied with regards to the precise area covered, or selection criteria used. The idea for Thirsty Tours® books came about, after I had written many reviews on TripAdvisor, I thought it was high time to create the first book, which soon turned into an idea for the series. Added to which, I lived in North London from 1989 to 1999 and have been a regular customer in Central London ever since, so where better to start.

The Public House and Associated Definitions

The famous writer, Dr Samuel Johnson (1709 to 1784), made lasting contributions to English literature. He remained a devout Anglican, generous philanthropist, committed Tory and more importantly a keen frequenter of Central London pubs. Note his well-known statement, no doubt made in a crowded public house: "No Sir! There is nothing that has yet been contrived by man, by which so much happiness has been produced, as by a good tavern!"

Thanks to Dr Johnson and many others, the public house soon became the cornerstone of British history, tradition and welcome for residents and visitors alike. In fact, all who came from far and wide experienced their special character and atmosphere. I feel that great Central London pubs exemplify this best and allow us to celebrate their unique place in our culture. They have survived the Great Fire of London in 1666, the Blitz and ambitious property development over the years, not to mention the heavy wear and tear that pubs inevitably suffer due to extended trading.

Central London pubs evolved from a handful of the earliest examples of taverns in the 15th and 16th centuries. The role of these taverns was primarily to sell ale, and they flourished with the influx of merchants and traders to the capital. The development of the inn, characterised by the need for food and accommodation as well as ale, saw them grow in popularity right through to the early 19th century, including with the rise of the coaching inn. These were often large and elegant establishments, which unfortunately went out of fashion with the advent of the railways.

The Licensing Act of 2003, which became effective from 2005, led to more flexible opening hours and removed previously arcane and restrictive laws, placing them under local authority control. The smoking ban, which took effect from July 2007, also changed peoples' drinking habits significantly. It also prompted the kind of refurbishments, which enabled pubs to appeal to a wider and some would say more discerning clientele. Pubs have been forced to adapt to the digital age, where customers feel the need to check their smartphones on average, every 12 minutes. They have also risen to the challenge of attracting everyone's critical interest, as the targets of customers' written reviews on the likes of TripAdvisor and other online forums.

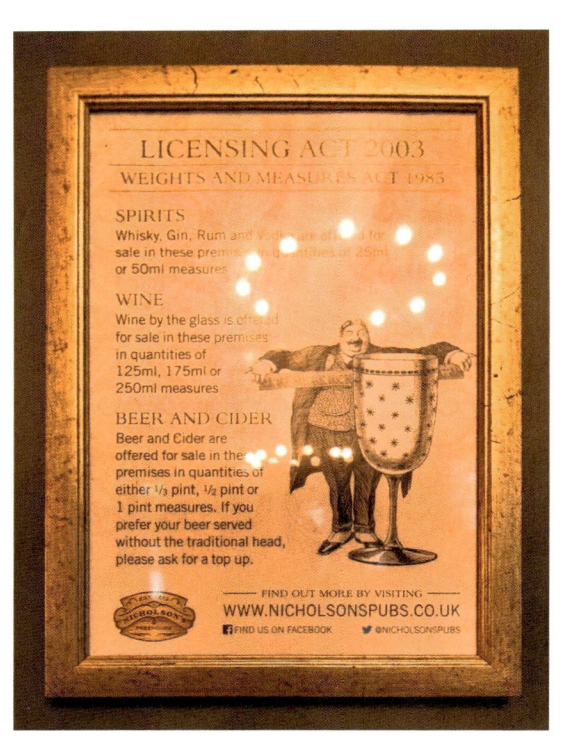

Reproduced with permission from
The Cambridge, 93 Charing Cross Rd,
WC2H 0DP

Definitions of Central London

Central London is the innermost part of London, England. The inner London boroughs were defined by the London Government Act 1963, and the definition is used for purposes such as the local government finance system, as they correspond to the former area of the County of London.

It appears that there is otherwise no clear consensus view on what truly constitutes Central London. Zone 1 of the London Underground seems to be the one most frequently used, as an informal answer to this question. Planners divide London formally into Central, Inner and Outer, although Central London is defined in the London Plan as the Central Activities Zone. This is officially the part of Inner London embracing certain boroughs, although transport planners treat the boroughs individually.

London Underground - The Circle Line

For the purpose of a book involving great pubs, it seems only fitting to define Central London as everything contained within the Circle line. This has been represented by the yellow line on the map of the London Underground since 1987 and, taken in isolation, looks like a bottle lying on its side, therefore entirely appropriate.

The Circle Line of the London Underground started operating in 1863. Originally 17 miles' long, with 27 stations, it now includes the spur from Edgware Road to Hammersmith, added in 2009. If this was a proper circle, it would cover an area of some 27 square miles, all situated north of the River Thames.

The current map of the London Underground is an evolution of the first map of London's rapid transit network, designed by Harry Beck in 1931. Beck worked for London Underground and found that, because the railway ran mostly underground, the physical locations of the stations were largely irrelevant to travellers, who just wanted to know how to get from one place to another.

Approach to the Selection of the 50 Greatest Pubs

Selecting the 50 greatest pubs, involved three key criteria:

1) Historical Interest

Each pub's impact on society over the years, perhaps through its involvement with famous events, or significant patrons frequenting its premises. Many good stories are anecdotal but they have been researched as far as possible to confirm their accuracy and source. Where this has not proved possible, a note appears in the review. Historical interest has been the main focus for selection.

2) Building and Architectural Significance

A public house has always been a key and generally central point of the community, or area within which it is located. This means the relevance of the physical building and premises linked to the historical significance, as it has traded over the years. Therefore, only pubs are included, that trade as a traditional "tavern" with access directly from street level.

Much of the great architecture of Central London was constructed in Georgian and Victorian times, then developed extensively over subsequent years. As times have changed and consumer tastes evolved, many great buildings have swapped usage, allowing recently established, popular chains to invest greatly in re-developing attractive properties, previously used by banks, government or other public bodies.

3) Entertainment and Leisure

The public house has also been the cornerstone of British culture for many hundreds of years and supports the social and often work-life of Londoners. Additionally, of course, the London pub provides extensive opportunities for visitors, as London welcomes some 20 million visitors each year. Each pub has been assessed, taking into account its importance as a location for rest, relaxation and social activity, whilst adhering to licensing laws, and reflecting changing consumer trends and expectations.

In particular, recent changes in tastes have been seen where pubs increasingly serve food as well as traditional wet sales. The rise of craft beer has extended offerings from multiple, recently established, independent breweries. Expectations have also changed in that everyone seems to demand free Wifi being available at all times.

The 50 Greatest Pubs in Central London

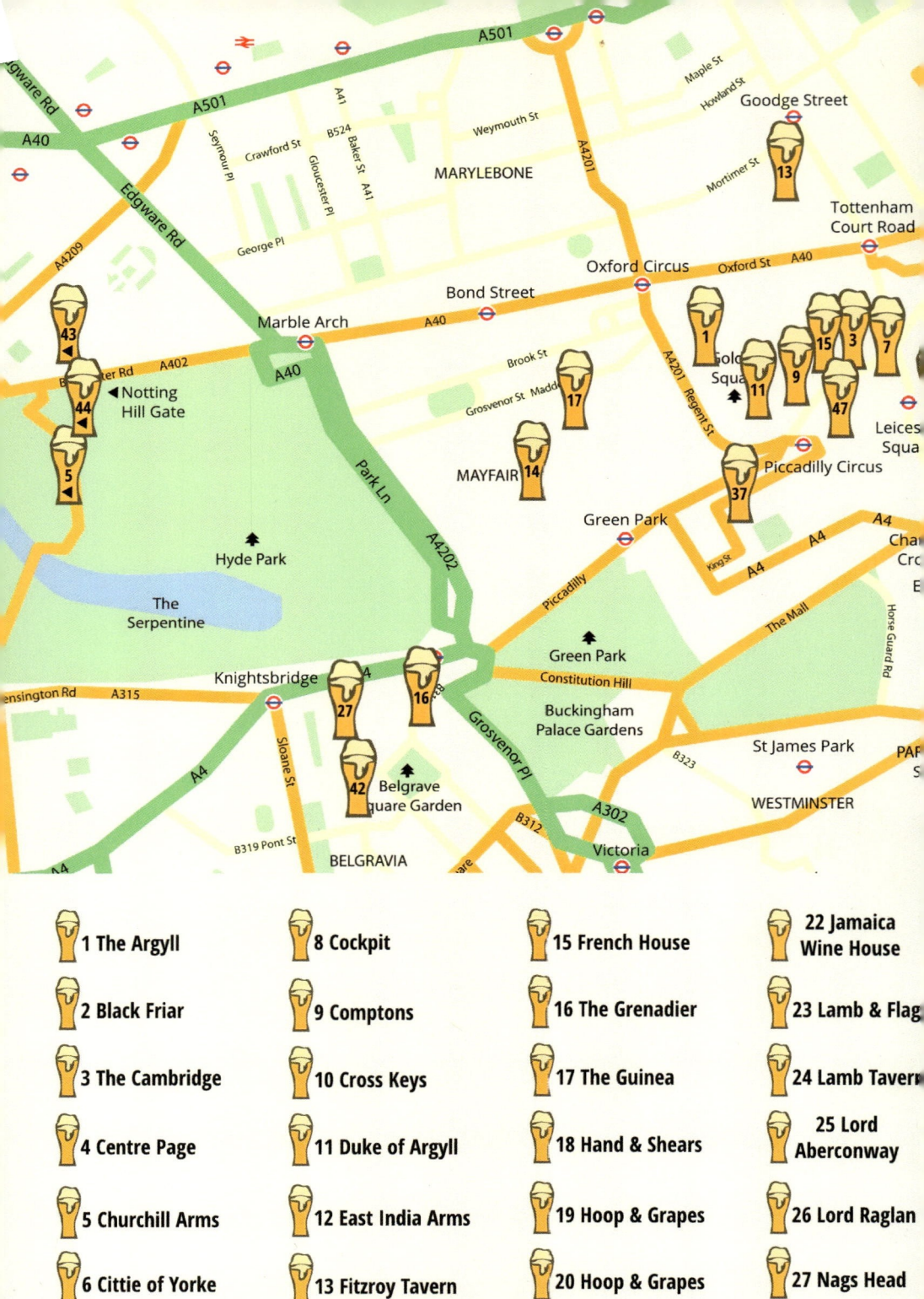

#	Pub	#	Pub	#	Pub	#	Pub
1	The Argyll	8	Cockpit	15	French House	22	Jamaica Wine House
2	Black Friar	9	Comptons	16	The Grenadier	23	Lamb & Flag
3	The Cambridge	10	Cross Keys	17	The Guinea	24	Lamb Tavern
4	Centre Page	11	Duke of Argyll	18	Hand & Shears	25	Lord Aberconway
5	Churchill Arms	12	East India Arms	19	Hoop & Grapes	26	Lord Raglan
6	Cittie of Yorke	13	Fitzroy Tavern	20	Hoop & Grapes	27	Nags Head
7	Coach & Horses	14	The Footman	21	The Hope	28	Nell Gwynne

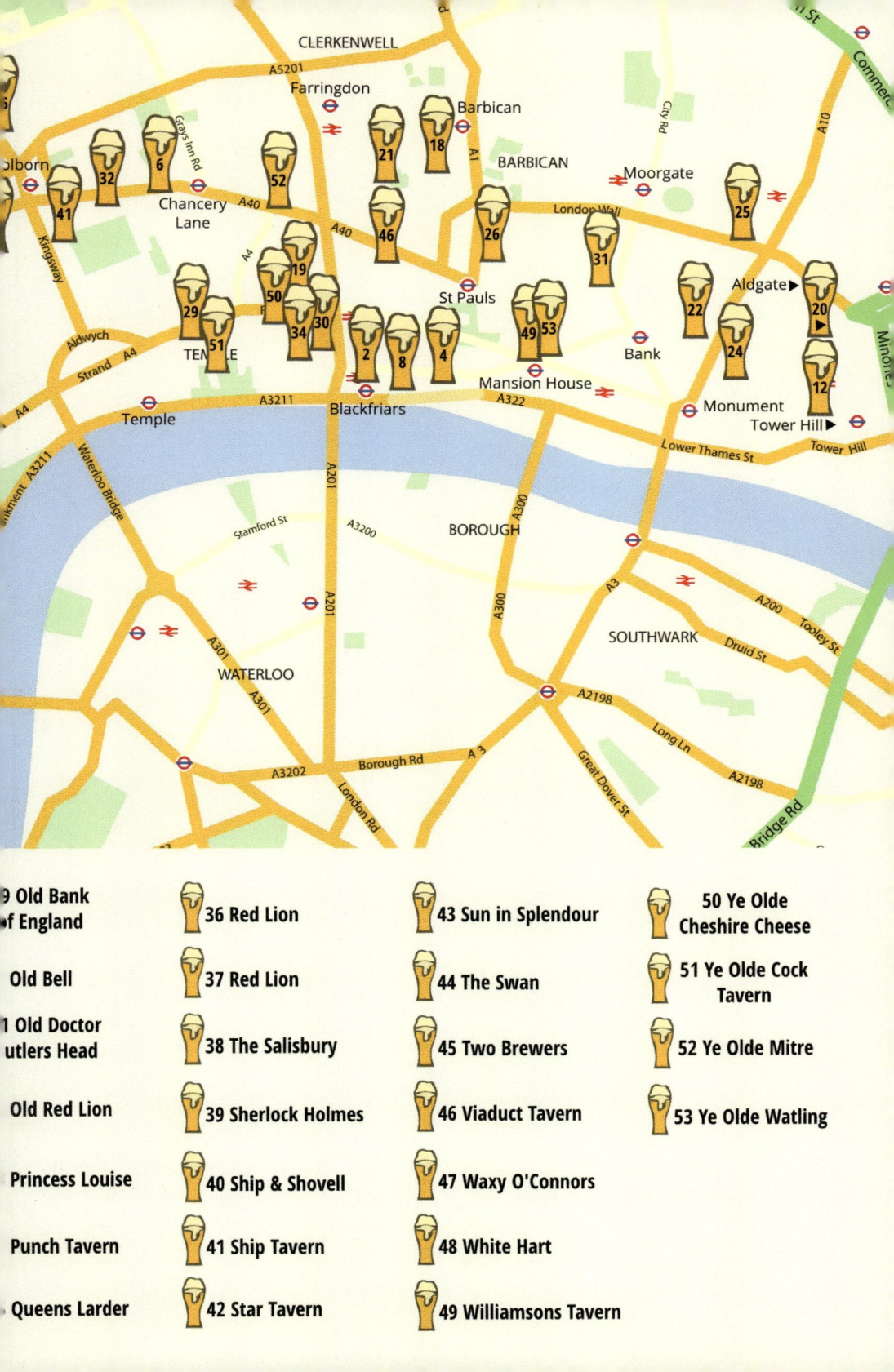

9 Old Bank of England	36 Red Lion	43 Sun in Splendour	50 Ye Olde Cheshire Cheese
Old Bell	37 Red Lion	44 The Swan	51 Ye Olde Cock Tavern
1 Old Doctor utlers Head	38 The Salisbury	45 Two Brewers	52 Ye Olde Mitre
Old Red Lion	39 Sherlock Holmes	46 Viaduct Tavern	53 Ye Olde Watling
Princess Louise	40 Ship & Shovell	47 Waxy O'Connors	
Punch Tavern	41 Ship Tavern	48 White Hart	
Queens Larder	42 Star Tavern	49 Williamsons Tavern	

The Argyll

> **Well-located in theatre land, late Victorian-era pub, with highly ornate and authentic interior, including snob screens and restaurant area. Now operates as a speciality fish house.**

This pub was built in 1742, opposite the site of the 2nd Duke of Argyll's London mansion, where the Palladium Theatre now stands. In former times, a tunnel linked both pub and mansion, to facilitate the Duke's ease of access. This building and an earlier Argyll Arms, dating from 1716, were torn down and the present building erected around 1866. As it was close to Oxford Street, at the northern-most edge of Soho and closely associated with the social development of this area, the pub thrived through Victorian times. Intense competition arose amongst the numerous hostelries, as they fought to attract business and residential customers in this rapidly expanding market.

A lavish refurbishment and conversion started in 1895, led by Robert Sawyer, one of the leading designers of the period. Sawyer spent significant money on his extensive works, transforming particularly the interior of the pub, with great attention to detail, creating a stunning looking environment. The entrance to the pub, on the far left hand side leads into a tiled corridor, with much use of marble and mahogany and a variety of cut glass mirrors, all providing a very positive first impression.

Victorians were obsessed with class and this explains the invention of snob screens, which were subsequently copied to become standard fixtures in many other London pubs. The Argyll is one of the best preserved, late Victorian era pubs, with elegant and highly polished wooden snug areas, effectively private spaces for class conscious customers, located the entire length of the mahogany bar.

Snob screens provided privacy, by virtue of their etched and engraved glass panels situated in the snug areas. These screens extended above normal head height, so customers could not easily be seen, but did not prevent their swift service by the bar staff when required. This all appealed greatly to sophisticated ladies, men of the church and other figures of authority, who could maintain liaisons in a discreet manner, unobserved by the masses and retaining the privacy they demanded.

The Argyll's close proximity to the shopping areas of Oxford Street, makes the pub a welcome retreat for weary shoppers. Also, located hard by the Palladium Theatre, means theatre goers have a useful meeting place. A dining area, separated from the drinking-only snug areas at the front, has been created at the back of the pub and continues upstairs on the first floor.

This dining area affords the customer a wonderful view of ornate plaster ceilings, and wall coverings deeply embossed in the Lincrusta style. This was invented by Frederick Walton in 1860, who also patented linoleum wall covering. Together with the many mirrors and other decorative details, the Argyll offers a real taste of the grandeur of late Victorian interior design, often dark in colour, but in this case truly authentic.

The pub is now part of the Nicholson's chain, and described as a speciality fish house, with dining rooms offering restaurant style service, providing both a formal and more relaxed dining experience. An extensive menu is available with a wide range of fare, including afternoon tea. The pub is proud to serve cask ales, including local beers, fine wines and in particular likes to draw attention to its extensive whisky and gin collection.

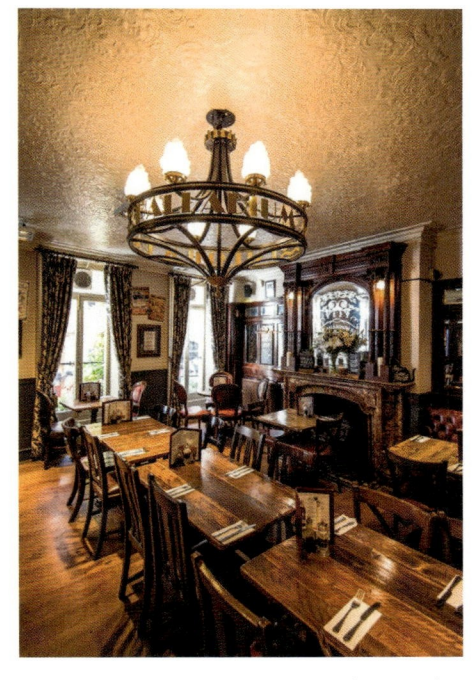

174 Queen Victoria Street, Victoria, EC4V 4EG

Black Friar

> A pub with a long and rich history, unique Art Nouveau architecture and elaborate interior depicting friars and carved motos, which was fortunately saved from demolition during the 1960's.

This pub was built on the site of London's former Dominican friary, in the Parish of Ludgate, originating in 1279. King Edward I gave permission for the friary to be built and visited it regularly, particularly using it for state occasions. The Dominicans were known as "Blackfriars" because of their distinctive black cloaks. When the Monasteries were dissolved during the Reformation in 1539, in the reign of Henry VIII, there were only 15 friars remaining and little is known of their fate. A significant amount of gold and silver was however recovered at this time, apparently ending up in the King's coffers.

The pub as it stands today, was originally constructed in 1875, then subsequently re-modelled by the architect Herbert Fuller-Clark, in the early 1900's, employing the anglicized, Art Nouveau style. This was during a period of decline in the London pub market, meaning only a very few other examples still survive. The improvements were co-ordinated by the then landlord, Alfred Pettitt. The first Black Friar pub stood at the centre of a group of buildings, linked by narrow passages. Demolition of these revealed a striking, wedge-shaped structure, which now faces directly across to Blackfriars station. The statue of a jovial looking friar, perched atop the front entrance makes it a famous landmark, and the narrow frontage is styled as a mock baronial hall.

Several powerful literary figures, including Sir John Betjeman, were key in leading a tireless campaign ensuring that the pub itself was not demolished to make way for a new road in the 1960's. Fortunately it has become a Grade 1 listed building, which means it should escape such threats from now on.

The interior was designed by the sculptor Henry Poole, who was heavily influenced by the Arts and Crafts movement, possibly created by the 19th century architect and designer, Augustus Pugin. Effigies of black coated, jovial looking and generally chubby friars are dotted everywhere, many of them appearing to be over indulging in various activities and certainly not the normal scene expected in a pub. One is even crawling along on his hands and knees. There is a massive fireplace and an ornate archway, leading into a small room at the back. The ceiling is decorated with mosaic and 50 different types of marble are on display throughout the building.

Various panels and pictures of friars adorn the walls, including one depicted sleeping, whilst surrounded by what appear to be fairies and devils. A sequence of messages is displayed around the copper reliefs with such reminders as: "Silence is golden"; "Haste is slow"; "Industry is all"; instructions such as "Don't advertise it, tell a gossip" and other historical words of wisdom. One copper relief depicts friars fishing, alongside the message: "Tomorrow will be Friday" and another has friars gardening, captioned as: "Saturday afternoon".

The sign above the partition, between the two parts of the bar, suggests that this was the site of the meeting in 1532, of the Holy Roman Emperor Charles V, the Papal Legate and King Henry VIII to debate the dissolution of his marriage to Catherine of Aragon. Nowadays, the pub is slightly different being a Nicholson's pub and described as a speciality sausage and chop house, with cask and craft ales also on offer for the modern drinker.

In the summer, happy drinkers overflow outside to join the jolly friar on the terrace, overlooking the traffic. Given the unique attractions of the Black Friar, a little traffic is certainly no barrier to the enjoyment of its clientele. No doubt Henry VIII would still have appreciated it all greatly.

93 Charing Cross Rd, Soho, WC2H 0DP

The Cambridge

Well-located pub, steeped in history, situated in the heart of theatre land, attracting a varied clientele and renowned as the perfect place for watching the rich variety of Central London life.

The Cambridge pub benefits from one main advantage, which is, as the saying goes: location, location, location. It stands at the intersection of Charing Cross Road and Shaftesbury Avenue, in the heart of London's West End theatre land, to be precise, Soho. The area takes its name from a hunting call, and was formerly a royal hunting ground for King Henry VIII. Centuries later, the cholera outbreak of 1854, caused many residents to leave and the area declined in popularity, until attracted by the cheap rents, artists and writers found homes amongst the many pubs and brothels, which had sprung up in the narrow streets.

The Cambridge stands on the site of the original Kings Arms, built in 1887, next to the Palace Theatre, formerly known as the Royal English House. Given its fine location, the pub's management prefer to offer a simple environment, furnished with plain wooden tables and chairs, and a collection of small, cushioned benches and partitions. This is complemented by the printed wallpaper, providing a somewhat regal feel in contrast with the bare floorboards. This is very much a standing room only place during regular busy periods, where you can admire the gold and black ceiling and elaborate light fittings. There is some respite from the small, bustling, ground floor bar area, with the more relaxed atmosphere of the first floor's Four Seasons dining area, although you will probably need to book to make sure you can be seated.

The pub opens all day, and the menu is typical of the Nicholson's chain that owns and operates it. A pre-theatre menu is prominently advertised, consisting of classic main dishes and delicious sharing plates. There is a framed summary of the life and times of the founder William Nicholson, an English distiller and Liberal party politician, who sat in the House of Commons for two periods, between 1866 and 1885, and later joined the Conservative party. He was also an accomplished first-class cricketer and became associated with the Marylebone Cricket Club, before turning to pubs on the acquisition of Three Mills in 1872. They moved production of its Lamplighter gin to a new location at this time, but it was forced to cease during World War 2.

The pub, slightly surprisingly, features on www.afternoontea.co.uk where its website states it is a spot to enjoy a relaxed and traditionally prepared afternoon tea, served with a generous helping of British hospitality. This is very welcome, especially in such a prime and busy location, where you would not usually expect to find this. The pub's website also describes it as a fantastic venue for a party, meeting or any celebratory event, which can be handled with a personal and professional approach to ease the headache of having to organise it oneself. Useful if you are looking for such facilities in a convenient, Central London location.

The clientele is understandably varied, with elegantly dressed pre- and post-theatre crowds, mixing with tourists and some local business people, ensuring it is lively and always interesting. This is clearly an excellent place to indulge in the old-fashioned art of people-watching, particularly if you are fortunate enough to be able to sit down at one of the tables, to observe customers inside, whilst also watching those passing by outside. This reflects the welcome extended to all comers. The numbers do dwindle as the evening wears on, as everyone heads off home, or on to other delights.

The pub has a most attractive copy of the Licensing Act of 2003, which all pubs have to display, of course, this one being noticeable for its humorous cartoon. There is an equally amusing cartoon imploring you to please watch your bags, which is sensible advice indeed.

Centre Page

A great survivor from the Blitz, close to St Paul's Cathedral, with a wealth of interesting Dickensian history and wider literary connections, also featuring in the works of Samuel Pepys.

The streets around St Pauls suffered enormously during the Blitz, so this pub is a rarity. Not only did it survive the bombing, by virtue of its position in a row of buildings, which the German planes miraculously overlooked, it also survived attempts to demolish it in 1967, after a successful campaign to save it. All in all, The Centre Page remains one of the oldest alehouses in London.

Reference books carry records of a Horn Alehouse in this vicinity from the 1660's, although that building was destroyed, like the majority of its neighbours, in the Great Fire of 1666. The pub has been rebuilt and altered on several occasions, whilst still retaining a strong connection with free-masonry dating from a period around the 1750's. The "Life and Times" of The Centre Page are described on the pub's website, showing it was formerly known as the Horn Tavern, then the Horn Coffee House, then the Bugell. It is said that Guy Fawkes had many a meeting in the cellar of the Horn Coffee House.

The pub also has strong connections with Charles Dickens, who knew this area well. As the Horn Coffee House, it features briefly in The Pickwick Papers. Mr Pickwick liked a drink and when incarcerated in the nearby Fleet Prison, he was often visited by his friends Winkle, Snodgrass and Tupman, who would arrange for a messenger to pop out and pick up a bottle or two of very good wine, from the Horn Coffee House, to help make Mr Pickwick's stay a little more bearable.

Samuel Pepys, no less, wrote about the Horn Tavern, in The Complete Diary of Samuel Pepys dated 13th April 1663, where he noted: "And so I called at the wardrobe on my way home, and there spoke at the Horn Tavern with Mr Moore a word or two". The Horn Tavern, or Coffee House, was again mentioned as a place where the Freemasons, or the "Free and Easy under the Rose" Society as it was known then, held their lodge meetings, the earliest recorded of which took place in 1754.

For some odd reason, given its rich history, the pub changed its name as recently as 2002 to The Centre Page, presumably due to its proximity to Fleet Street. The previous name is acknowledged on the current sign, which states "Formerly the Horn Tavern" and refers to the strong Dickens' connection. The old saloon bar was once dominated by a bust of the great man, subsequently replaced by a more recent celebrity, a signed photograph of David Hasselhoff, the singer and star of the TV series, Baywatch.

The menu in the pub is described as 'traditional modern British, with a passionate kitchen team.' Diners can choose to sit in either the booths, adjoining the bar, or in the downstairs dining room, the Boardroom, or indeed the Dickens Room. Weather permitting, the outside patio area is also an excellent spot to dine, while overlooking St Paul's Cathedral, and is but a short distance from the Millennium Bridge over the Thames. The pub's website has been produced in the style of a newspaper and includes details of special offers and forthcoming events. This real British pub is clearly a great survivor.

119 Kensington Church Street, Notting Hill Gate, W8 7LN

Churchill Arms

> Renowned for its long-established Thai restaurant, exterior floral displays and eccentric memorabilia, mostly based on Sir Winston Churchill, Prime Ministers and Presidents, plus an extensive butterfly collection.

The pub was built in 1750 and is renowned for its style and features, with an attractive exterior on a parade of luxury shops, as befits this part of Central London. A truly impressive floral display covers the outside of the building. Plants and flowers blaze forth from some 100 tubs, 42 hanging baskets and 48 window boxes at a cost of close to £25,000 per annum. The pub has the honour of being one of the very few to win awards at the world-famous Chelsea Flower Show.

Come December, 90 Christmas trees and 20,000 fairy lights join the floral display, to encourage Londoners to get into the Christmas spirit and it is hard to walk past without stepping through the welcoming door, into a pub with this much vibrancy and illumination. The decorative exterior is all down to the Churchill Arms' legendary landlord Gerry O'Brien. They celebrated 30 years of the tradition back in July 2015, and it is still going strong to this day.

The pub was originally called the Marlborough, after Sir Winston Churchill's Grandfather, John Spencer-Churchill, The 7th Duke of Marlborough, who was elected Member of Parliament for Woodstock, twice, within the period 1844 to 1857. Together with his wife, Lady Frances, he frequented the establishment in the 1800s, along with a host of other famous visitors. The pub was renamed after the end of the Second World War, in honour of Sir Winston, Britain's wartime Prime Minister. Strangely, all references to the Duke of Marlborough seem to have vanished, even though their ancestor, the first Duke, succeeded in winning the Battle of Blenheim for the nation in 1704.

Presently owned and operated by Fullers Brewery, many original features have been lovingly preserved inside the pub. Original snob screens remain to the left of the bar and the whole of the pub is divided into distinct areas. It is clear that it was originally designed as three sections, each with its own doorway to the street.

The interior glows with open fires, candles and amber lights and is packed with Churchill memorabilia, as the main theme on display but by no means the only one. A variety of wall plaques bear the great man's most memorable quotes, including everyone's favourite: "We will fight them on the beaches, we will never surrender". Books written by him and about him can be removed from the shelves and browsed, whilst enjoying the other considerable delights of the visit. These include references to a selection of other British Prime Ministers, from Robert Walpole to Harold Wilson et al, which occupy an entire wall.

On the other side of the pub, a similar display recognises American Presidents from Nixon to Washington. The truly British eccentric approach is also evident in the Presidents' area, which for some reason also contains a variety of potties hanging from the ceiling, possibly to remind gentlemen that their lavatories are located nearby.

By complete contrast, another distinct display appears in yet another area of the pub. Beautiful baskets and a collection of some 1,600 butterflies, mounted and framed, obviously with great care and dedication, appear alongside lanterns, pots and hat boxes, and various items hanging from the ceiling.

The Churchill Arms is celebrated as the first London pub to serve Thai food. It has a butterfly-themed, conservatory dining area, the entrance to which carries the sign "Operations Room", as a further nod to Churchill's wartime achievements. For over 25 years, the chefs in the Thai kitchen have been delighting their guests with authentic flavours of Thailand and appealing to a broad range of tastes. For additional entertainment, the pub screens regular live international sports events.

22 High Holborn, Holborn, WC1V 6BN

Cittie of Yorke

> Cavernous pub built in the 1920's with extensive and characterful features, including an unusual fireplace, long bar and wooden booths. Previously known in the days of Dylan Thomas as Henekey's bar.

It is claimed that a pub or alehouse has traded on this site since around 1430. If this is true and if the original building still stood, it would rank as the oldest pub in London. However, it seems to have appeared in a variety of guises over the centuries. Today the Citie of York with its impressive exterior, fine architecture and ancient clock, closely resembles a medieval coaching inn.

In the 17th century, the building housed one of the many coffee houses, which were fashionable at the time and where no alcohol was served. This omission may well have brought about the swift re-design of the place into a traditional tavern, serving many a fine ale, to broaden its appeal to 18th century Londoners.

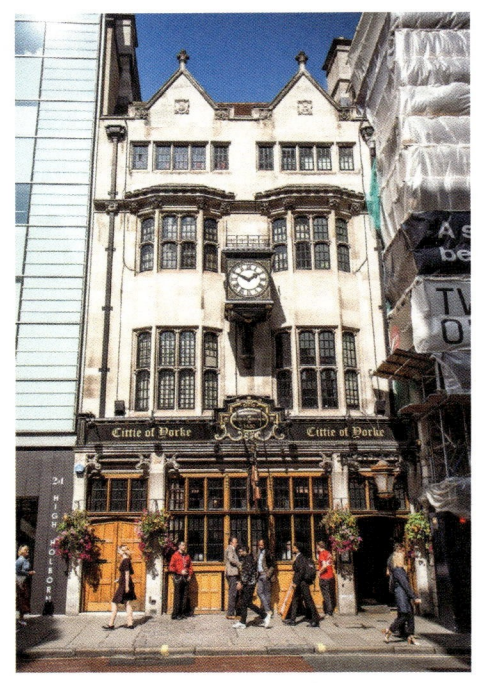

Early in the 20th century, the Cittie of Yorke stood as an example of distinctive Victorian modernism, reflected in its interior features of etched glass, mahogany and mirrors, as found in any good gin palace of the time. Then in the 1920s, it underwent a complete rebuild and makeover, to re-emerge as something more befitting the Tudor era, filled with historic themes, in complete contrast to contemporary trends in pub décor. It's possible the owners were trying to create something truly unique, soon after the end of the First World War. They succeeded in creating a front elevation resembling that of Hampton Court Palace.

In 1951, one of the finest Welsh poets, Dylan Thomas, sat in the corner of Henekey's long bar in Holborn and wrote an impromptu, although famous poem simply entitled "Song", presumably aided by a glass in his hand. The beginning of the poem reads "This little song was written in Henekey's long bar High Holborn". Henekey's is now known as the Cittie of Yorke, having been renamed by its present owners Samuel Smith's Breweries in 1979. This new name was adopted from another old pub nearby, which is no longer trading.

The main bar remains the key attraction, claiming to be one of the longest in Britain, where a stunning interior was designed to resemble the great hall of a Tudor mansion. This has a high pitched, vaulted ceiling, rather like a timbered church. A row of seven carrels or snugs are on one side of the bar, with three more on the opposite wall, offering complete and welcome privacy, often described as "nooks and crannies".

There are snug bars to be found in earlier pubs and it appears that this was copied from Victorian designs. In the centre of the bar area stands an unusual triangular-shaped fireplace, dating from the late Georgian or Regency era, although with no apparent chimney, rather seeming to involve an elaborate system where smoke is drawn down and outside.

Above the long bar area are rows of massive oak wine barrels. They appear to be much larger than the standard wine tun, which holds 216 imperial gallons. These may or may not have had a real use as storage vessels, given that it would have been almost impossible to move them, especially if filled.

During the week, the Cittie of Yorke attracts customers primarily from the legal profession, in view of its close proximity to Holborn and Lincoln's Inn, where many chambers are located. It is listed in CAMRA's National Inventory of Historic Pub Interiors. This is reflected in the ethos of serving good beer, with the pub having a well-deserved excellent reputation for offering good value for its drinks and food.

Cockpit

> Georgian pub with a colourful past, including hosting cock fights. It has close connections to Shakespeare, who apparently lived nearby, and was rebuilt in its present form in 1897.

The narrow streets and lanes leading up to the City of London, from Queen Victoria Street, maintain a medieval formation, which gives this area considerable charm, within the old square mile. The pub is tucked away in St Andrew's Hill, only a stone's throw from St Paul's Cathedral. This remains very much an old school pub, allowing you to relax and take a step back in time. A public house has been on this site, perched at the junction of Ireland Yard, since at least the 16th century. Keep an eye out for the ornate entrance to Apothecaries Hall, as you pass by, en route to the pub.

This is one of a number of London locations with associations to William Shakespeare and of all of them, Ireland Yard is by far the best documented. It is believed he owned a house nearby. Although now just a small alley, Shakespeare would have seen it as being rather grander in his day, due to the fact it constituted the main entrance to Blackfriars Monastery. It was here that buildings were seized and sold off during the dissolution, although they were fortunately left intact. The former gatehouse was purchased by Shakespeare in 1613 for £140, apparently in partnership with actors, to use as what became known as Blackfriars Playhouse.

When the pub was known as the Cock Pit, then two separate words, it was famous for hosting cockfights and gambling, until this so-called sport was banned in 1849. At this time the pub changed its name to the Three Castles, most likely due to the fact that it was near to the site of Baynard Castle, which was closed from the 15th century and ended up being destroyed in the Great Fire of 1666.

The pub underwent a major refurbishment in 1970, after which it adopted the name the Cockpit, as one word. The present building dates from around 1830 and enjoyed improvement works in the 1890's, including the installation of a small gallery, surrounding the bar. The corner entrance doors are semi-circular, divided at the centre and painted in elegant, if somewhat faded, black and gold, with solid glass panels. Signs alongside the main door warn customers not to enter if wearing soiled clothing or dirty boots, because they will not be served.

The interior is otherwise very well worn, with original 1970's radiators, crimson velvet and a small curved bar, slightly elevated from the rest of the pub. The gallery, which is no longer open to the public, displays memorabilia, such as jugs suspended from its railings and as one might expect, paintings depicting cock fights, as well as what appears to be a stuffed example of an original contestant.

All in all, the Cockpit is more reminiscent of an East End local, and, un-usually for a City pub, it is open on Saturdays and Sundays, no doubt due to its popularity among the bell ringers of nearby St Paul's Cathedral, where it is also open on Good Friday.

The pub is the proud owner of a rare shove-ha'penny board, where bar staff will lend you the old pennies. Local customers, many descended from earlier regulars, will no doubt be willing to show you how it works and explain the rules, such as they are.

Comptons

> The Grand Dame of Soho, serving the gay community for decades, a beautiful pub with lavish decorations, loads of atmosphere and a host of regular events.

Comptons occupies an attractive building, erected in 1890, designed by architects W.A. Williams and Hopton and established originally as the Swiss Hotel. Williams and Hopton exhibited their design for the Swiss Hotel at the Royal Academy, which resulted in an illustration of the building being published in "The Builder" on 25th October 1890. This would have represented quite an accolade, given the sheer number of new buildings being completed in Central London during the late Victorian era.

By the 1950's the Swiss Hotel had been renamed the Swiss Tavern. It soon acquired a reputation for attracting a gay clientele, although understandably an unofficial one, given the laws restricting gay lifestyles at the time. Success followed and by 1986 the Swiss Tavern had been renovated and renamed Comptons of Soho, as a proud and openly gay bar. The substantial building it occupied was fully converted to licensed premises. In November 2006, it celebrated its 20th anniversary. QX magazine wrote a review, affectionately describing the pub as "The Grand Dame of Queer Street".

Located in the heart of Soho's gay village, this name appears to have stuck and is adopted by its lively clientele, who often refer to it as simply "The Grand Dame of Soho." It enjoys loyal support from its clientele and has become an integral part of London's gay scene. This is now actively promoted as Soho's favourite gay bar, extending a warm welcome to all and creating an excellent vibe. Very few would disagree with that.

Previously operated by the Faucet Inn Pub Company, it has recently been acquired by The Stonegate Pubs company, which has enthusiastically embraced their tradition of delivering fantastic customer experience. Stonegate operates over 690 pubs and bars across the UK, with a wide variety of formats, from community pubs, through branded bars, to country inns and late-night venues. Comptons of Soho sits proudly within their varied collection.

The interior of the pub has two bars. The ground floor area surrounds a horseshoe-shaped bar, popular with a varied gay male crowd, including many tourists. There is a lounge area upstairs, with a balcony from which you can watch the world go by and soak up the atmosphere, either with friends or going alone.

The interior decorations are suitably lavish, with chandeliers, candelabra, an elegant old clock and a piano. It's the kind of environment which may well have appealed to Liberace, especially if invited to play the piano and perform. However, there is, unfortunately, no evidence of his appearing here, except perhaps in spirit.

The pub markets itself as the ideal place to hold birthday parties, works do's, hen nights, or just a get together, guaranteeing a great time whatever the occasion. Posters displayed around the pub encourage booking a space, with party packages available. They cater to everyone's tastes with a wide selection of drinks on offer, including two ale hand pumps with craft beers and lagers. There is a Manic Monday club with resident DJ and attractively priced drinks packages, designed to liven up the start of the traditional working week.

31 Endell Street, Covent Garden, WC2H 9BA

Cross Keys

Cosy, classic old London boozer, with ornate frontage, including floral displays, and stacks of character with an eccentric collection of memorabilia packed into the small bar area.

The Cross Keys was built in 1848, in an area off Endell Street, the street being named after a rector of St Giles-in-the-Field Church. The pub building arose from slum clearance works, carried out at the time to help improve these abjectly poor areas, where life expectancy for the residents was shockingly low. Overlooking the clearance work, stood the infamous St Giles and St George Workhouse, where many of those from the slums ended up. Conditions in the workhouses were appalling, which led to an article being printed in the medical journal, The Lancet, that shocked Londoners of the time. The pub was built to serve the local community and still maintains a genuinely local feel, attracting everyone from office workers to theatre-goers and beyond.

The front of the pub is adorned with a majestic floral display, creating a fragrant and colourful welcome at the doorway. The display is maintained all year round, adding to the local appeal. The Cross Keys became famous during the First World War, when two well-known suffragette doctors, Flora Murray and Louisa Garrett Anderson, decided they wanted to help treat the thousands of wounded soldiers. The women originally offered their services to the French Government and after experiencing some local resistance, were eventually allowed to open a military hospital in the Hotel Claridge in Paris, followed by a second in Wimereux on the Boulogne coast.

Having learnt the essential skills needed to treat war injuries, the two women were invited to open their own hospital in London. The dilapidated old infirmary of the former workhouse in Endell Street, opposite the Cross Keys, was provided as the site for the hospital, which gained financial support from the Royal Army Medical Corps. Very quickly, the many injured servicemen started to arrive in Endell Street. Over 24,000 patients were treated in the hospital, which was staffed entirely by women. During the war, The Cross Keys pub became the social centre of the community, as a haven for recuperating patients and other servicemen returning from the front.

The pub has retained its local feel and remains a traditional public house, resisting any suggestions to change its integrity and style. As more and more themed pubs and bars appear, it does look a little out of place in Covent Garden, more like a rural village pub, covered in flowers with marble columns and two cherubs sitting atop the sign bearing its name.

The owner of the pub is an antiques dealer, which has no doubt led to the vast collection of bizarre memorabilia covering the interior walls. There is a napkin, autographed by Elvis Presley, and a cricket bat, autographed by Sir Don Bradman, the legendary Australian cricketer. There are also deep-sea divers' helmets, other copper items hanging from the ceiling and shoals of stuffed fish. More recently the collection has welcomed Beatles' memorabilia, including an attractive bust of John Lennon.

The lighting inside the pub is diffused and quite low, which takes time to get used to when coming in from bright sunshine. This definitely enhances the impression of entering an old London pub, with richly-coloured furnishings and upholstery, not to mention the diverse artefacts on display. Upstairs, a cosy function room is available for hire, complete with its own bar, which gives an excellent view of the hustle and bustle in Endell Street.

Duke of Argyll

Soho-based institution with traditional approach and reputation for service, whilst demonstrating an old world and slightly edgy feel with well restored bar including Victorian style snug areas.

This pub is centrally located in Soho, at the junction of Great Windmill Street and Brewer Street, two roads in from Shaftesbury Avenue. The exterior appears a little battered, which gives a sense of history and individual charm, particularly due to an earlier restoration, which accentuated its old world feel. This approach bucks the trend of its owners and operators Samuel Smiths brewery, the pub maintaining its own distinctive and non-corporate style of décor. The exterior sign has an attractive crest with the motto in Latin: "Ne Obliviscaris", which translates as Do Not Forget.

The interior downstairs has been lovingly restored and comprises a number of snugs within an area that is relatively small, creating a look of cramped clutter. The bar extends along the entire back of the pub, facilitating rapid service for customers who find themselves mostly relegated to standing room only.

The pit has wooden floors and is furnished with high stools, tables and columns for customers to rest against whilst enjoying a drink. The pub stands at the corner of two streets and its main doors lead directly out onto the pavement. This encourages many drinkers, during favourable weather, to gather outside and on a good day it looks as if there are more people drinking outside the pub, than in it.

It's possible to grab one of the armchairs clustered around the window areas, in order to sit down and relax in comfort, but you have to be either very quick at spotting them becoming vacant, or early enough to claim one first. This allows you to gaze up at the miniature opera house impression on the ceiling. Lower walls are more attractively covered in wallpaper that is again distinctly different from the pub operator's usual style. The old-world feel is enhanced by various historic posters and photos around the walls, including an architect's drawing and brief history, together with a biography of John Thomas Wimpers who designed this is 1885, who was also associated with the Grosvenor Estate.

The pub does retain its excellent reputation for great value, particularly in this otherwise notoriously expensive part of Central London, having perhaps a little more "oomph" than some other more mundane places. Due to its location, the pub attracts a huge variety of customers, drawn to the back streets of Soho. This is not however seedy, which you can feel slightly closer to Chinatown, with young and old, rich and poor, seemingly getting on well together. This befits the friendly feel to the pub, although everyone can see you are there, so not obviously a place for more intimate meetings.

The restaurant upstairs has a real fire in the fireplace, which creates an atmosphere that is warm and cosy. It serves a range of classic dishes from an extensive menu. This appears reasonably priced although not necessarily an ideal place for a more relaxed restaurant style experience. Staff are renowned for their quick service and attention, particularly if a diner has any particular time pressures, for example with tickets to get to the start of a production at one of the many theatres close by. Tread carefully though if you are in a rush to pop to the toilets before leaving, as they are situated at the end of a steep, spiral stone staircase.

East India Arms

> Located next to the place where the East India Company had its headquarters when prominent, a traditional style, typical City pub, catering for commuters and tourists, inevitably mostly for standing.

The East India Company started in 1600 and traded until its demise in 1858, having been one of the most powerful commercial organisations in the world. It traded commodities including coffee, nutmeg, opium, tea and spices and monopolised the market until India was brought into the British Empire.

The pub stands on a site previously occupied by the Magpie Ale House, recorded from 1650, where the present pub dates from 1829 and is believed to be the oldest surviving building in the Lloyds's Avenue Conservation Area. It was built of warm red brick with a curved corner connecting the sides. The pub was so-named to commemorate the area's links with the East India Company, which started trading from rooms in nearby Philpot Lane. Employees of the company were probably the pub's earliest customers.

Following the impact of the Blitz and subsequent redevelopment, much of the Fenchurch Street area in London's modern financial heart has become dominated by bland office buildings, although this lovely old pub still survives, close to key tourist attractions, such as the Tower of London, a mere 10 minute walk away. All in all, a great spot for history hunters to pursue a trip down memory lane.

The Interior is just one room, with a single dark wood bar and large, arched windows. Vertical drinking is the order of the day unless you can secure one of the few barstools available. This is described on the pub's website as a blissfully traditional place to enjoy a pint in the City. It has authentic wooden floors and furnishings, with wonderfully nostalgic old photos on the walls, evoking images of supposedly happier times past.

The pub is now operated by Kent-based brewers Shepherd Neame, who claim to be Britain's oldest brewery, where their archives show they have been brewing in the market town of Faversham, possibly as early as 1570. They provide a link to the long-standing history of the pub by selling India Pale Ale and other great beers. The pub caters to a variety of tastes and provides a welcome escape from work in the local offices or the travails of sightseeing activities. Its close proximity to Fenchurch Street station, means many people simply drop in for some good old fashioned hospitality, whilst waiting for their train, or perhaps the train after that.

The pub's website states that they offer cracking cask ales and lagers, which come courtesy of Shepherd Neame, and there's a good selection of wines, ciders, spirits and soft drinks too. The site also includes quotes from customers on TripAdvisor including "glorious pub, a wonderful back street local, beer was excellent and their décor was great. Staff were efficient and helpful". One other customer describes this as being where to find the best Bishops Finger ale in London.

Like most of the pubs in The City, the East India Arms only opens Monday to Friday, although their website includes a helpful section to get in touch if you are feeling wistful outside of opening hours. You do, however, have to prove you are not a robot in doing so, how times have moved on since the great days of the East India Company. The name of the pub creates an unusual ordering of sites when you search online, be careful not to fall for suggestions to visit the majestic Agra fort or view the Taj Mahal in all its glory in India, unless of course you are inspired to visit these places to reflect on how it all came about.

Fitzroy Tavern

> A Fitzrovia legend, inspired by enterprising immigrants, and recently reconstructed from historic blueprints and photos, the pub has an old-fashioned Victorian style interior with intimate areas.

Fitzrovia is arguably the best known and longest-established of the artists' communities, which grew up in Central London from the 18th century. This area, situated adjacent to Tottenham Court Road was named after The Fitzroy, a renowned bohemian public house. The pub is located on Charlotte Street, regarded as the heart of Fitzrovia, with many restaurants and clubs, and was named after Queen Charlotte, the popular wife of King George III.

Originally constructed as the Fitzroy coffee house in 1883, it was converted into a pub in 1897 called The Hundred Marks, in view of the number of German immigrants, who had settled in the area. It was renamed the Fitzroy in 1919 by Judah "Pop" Kleinfield, a Polish-Russian immigrant, who became landlord at the time, having previously had a rather different career as a master tailor in Saville Row. The re-naming was influenced by the name of the Fitzroy family who owned much of the land on which Fitzrovia stands.

Charlotte Street became famous during the period spanning the 1920's through to the mid 1950's, as a meeting place for many of London's artists, intellectuals and bohemian individuals. They numbered such giants of literature as George Orwell and Dylan Thomas, who lived nearby, and included more recent visitors such as comedians Kenneth Williams and Tommy Cooper.

Judah Kleinfield subsequently passed the pub on to his daughter, Annie. She and her husband Charles Allchild also proved to be genial hosts, running the pub right through until 1956, when they bowed out following a legal battle. Augustus John was the last "member of Fitzrovia" until his death in 1961, and the pub has dedicated a wall of memorabilia to him as a tribute. Other famous local residents included artists' model Nina Hammett, the original Queen of Bohemia, and Tom Driberg, who coined the word 'Fitzrovia' in 1940.

Sally Fiber, the grand-daughter of Judah Kleinfield, worked behind the bar from a very young age and eventually wrote a history of the pub called "The Fitzroy - The Autobiography of a London Tavern", which was updated and re-published in September 2014.

The pub was closed for a complete re-build in 2018, now re-opened under the management of Samuel Smiths brewery. The quality of this recent refurbishment - based on archive photos as a Charrington's house - has been rightly recognised with a pub design award from CAMRA. It has iron pub signs erected in keeping with the original photos. The original Victorian appearance has also been revived on the ground floor, with polished mahogany partitions, wood panelling and etched glass, recreating original snugs around the semi island bar.

The story of the pub is displayed on the walls, with paintings, posters, photos and other memorabilia, including pictures of Dylan Thomas and Michael Bentine drinking there. The pub also makes an appearance in the high-resolution picture of London taken in 2012 as a part of the Cities 360 project, showing the most extensive panorama of London taken from the top of the BT Tower.

The pub has also been the home of the Pear Shaped Comedy Club since 2000, which appears every Wednesday night in the downstairs bar. The website for these events describes them as continuing regardless of football, wars, tsunamis, bird flu, swine flu, pandemics, earthquakes, credit crunches or un-employed bankers. It promises that the show will go on, even if there are no comics, audience, laughs or enthusiasm. This positive attitude is a great attraction to audiences, even if occasionally things may go a little awry, as one would expect from a club called Pear Shaped.

The Footman

> An elegant Mayfair institution, one of the oldest pubs in London, famous for its sign, traditional flag flying outside, formerly known as "The Only Running Footman" reflecting the previous ownership.

This is one of the oldest pubs in London, existing since 1749. It was originally called the Running Horse, a regular haunt of footmen, who served the fabulous households of Mayfair. The area soon established itself as one of the grandest places to reside in Central London.

Footmen were employed to run in front of their masters' coaches, to ensure a safe passage and, where necessary, pay any tolls in advance along the way. As motorised transport rapidly replaced the horse-drawn, one footman decided on a complete career change and bought the pub. How he managed to acquire the money for this can only be speculated upon, but it is presumed through honest endeavours. He promptly renamed the pub after himself and thus it became known as The Only Running Footman. With his former colleagues remaining as loyal customers, the pub became well known as a location to meet and exchange anecdotes of the day.

Subsequently, the name was shortened to simply The Footman and it remains a grand old three-storey pub and dining rooms, located beside Berkeley Square, in the beating heart of the prime residential area of Mayfair. The exterior retains its traditional style, with more modern touches introduced during a recent refurbishment, and the addition of an attractive flag pole flying the Union Jack, in celebration of its quintessential English heritage.

The interior reflects the long and extensive history of the pub, albeit with many modern twists and touches, which create a sense of timelessness. The single room bar area is elegantly furnished, resembling a drawing room of one the mansions close by. Here one can while away many hours in relaxing surroundings and observe the diverse crowd that frequent the pub. This includes many international visitors, attracted by the historical significance and appealing location, a leisurely 10 minute walk from the more frenetic Piccadilly, passing the Ritz Hotel and Green Park tube station.

The pub today is also well renowned for its pleasant dining experience, in the beautiful first floor restaurant, which is available for large groups, or what the pub describes as smaller soirees. This provides a quiet haven away from the hustle and bustle of the bar, filled in the evening with after work drinkers, and offers the chance to enjoy perhaps more romantic meals. Private parties can also be arranged in the Mount Room, a smaller space, along with the Mews room, perfect for more intimate dinners or break out meetings away from the office.

More extensive functions can be accommodated through hiring the whole shebang, which is marketed on the pub's website, as an opportunity to say you have commandeered your own personal pub for a day.

The superb dining is now a key feature of the pub, where seasonal ingredients are featured on delicious menus and customers enjoy excellent service. Their love of ales is not forgotten however, and they pride themselves on keeping an excellent selection on rotation. Four hand-pulls and eight keg lines showcase the best craft and international brews available. The pub's website has an extensive gallery section, which allows you to review the look and feel of the place before your visit. You can also see the original pub, on various old black and white photos showing Victorian era Mayfair and interior views, including up the stairs to the first floor.

French House

> Truly deserves its reputation as the best-known pub, in the naughtiest square mile, with rich and diverse French orientated history, although you still only get served beer in half pint glasses.

This looks nothing like a London pub, as all involved in its history have tried to keep it as closely resembling a bar in the backstreets of Paris as possible, including the prominent display of the tricolour outside. The pub's official name for the most part of the 20th century was The York Minster but began its inevitable transition to "The French", as it was more colloquially called, from 1914 onwards. The owner Berta Schmitt sold the business to a colourful chef, Victor Berlemont, who was also famous for sporting an enormous waxed moustache. He started to import wine from France in barrels, bottling it on the premises, which clearly helped to make the pub very popular with an increasingly arty clientele.

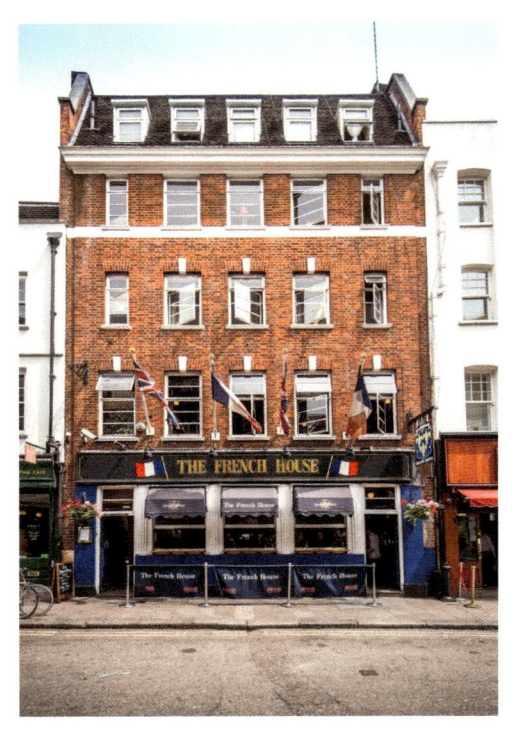

Victor, who was in fact Belgian, became the first foreigner to be granted a full licence to operate a pub in London. "The French" extended its reputation as a small corner of France, by hosting painters, writers, actors and particularly boxers, probably reflecting Victor's passion for the sport. George Carpenter, who fought and lost to Jack Dempsey in the 1921 world heavyweight championship, was a regular visitor. Apparently, a ring was erected in the basement for George to display his talents. Another regular Maurice Chevalier, the French actor and singer also liked to pop in for a glass of wine.

During the Second World War, the pub became a symbol of French resistance in London and home to the Free French. It is said that Charles de Gaulle visited and may possibly have written part of his famous radio speech, to rally his countrymen in June 1940, at a table in the restaurant upstairs.

Victor passed away in 1953, having seen The French through both World Wars.

His son Gaston took over, and he turned out to be even more flamboyant than his father, including growing an even grander moustache. This part of Soho was known as the home of bohemia in the 1950's and 1960's and the interior of the pub still reflects the era, its décor now a little tired although clearly still rich in Gallic charm. The clientele during Gaston's reign included actors, street performers and painters all of whom he readily befriended, not to mention many a young lady who sought sanctuary from the streets often late at night.

Gaston's downfall came as a result of his generosity, paying for many a taxi ride home for tired customers and extending credit to his regulars, to encourage them to return to his little corner of France. One famous story tells of a lady, who had wine thrown over her by her drunk escort, and to have Gaston step in and say "Why Madame, your glass is empty, let me refill it for you."

The barrister and author John Mortimer, famous for creating and writing the British TV series, Rumpole of the Bailey, was also a regular, as was Dylan Thomas, who famously left his only copy of "Under Milk Wood" under a chair, during one riotous evening. Gaston rescued it and returned it safely the next day. The event celebrating Gaston's retirement on Bastille Day in 1989 apparently, although perhaps not that surprisingly, caused the pavements around Dean Street to be littered with empty champagne bottles.

This all led to the pub finally becoming known as The French House, with all the old traditions maintained by Lesley Lewis, who succeeded Gaston as landlord. Very much a character too, Lesley has continued the pub's well-deserved reputation as a hip, although slightly faded, bohemian bar in a cool part of London, which still retains its undoubted Gallic charm. The pub still only serves beer in half pints, except on April Fool's day, when pints are served at the pub's annual fund-raiser. The French has a no mobile phone rule, which is fairly arbitrarily applied, if at all.

18 Wilton Row, Belgravia, SW1X 7NR

The Grenadier

One of the most attractive pubs in London in mews location, with military themes and many a tall tale involving Cedric the ghost, leading to an extensive collection of bank notes being left on the ceilings.

Looking like a village pub, with a vibrant red, white and blue exterior, The Grenadier stands amongst the affluent mews houses of Wilton Row, tucked away in the cobbled streets of Belgravia. This historic pub, built in 1720, has strong military connections and originally operated as the officers' mess for the First Royal Regiment of Foot Guards, whose barracks stood alongside. It was originally called the Guardsman, when it opened in 1818, later renamed The Grenadier. A striking feature is the bright red sentry box at the side of the steps, leading up to the entrance, quite unique in fact.

The Duke of Wellington, who commanded the forces that defeated Napoleon at Waterloo in 1815, may have visited, but what is certain is that the famous battle led to the Regiment being renamed, following a royal proclamation citing their outstanding bravery. They became the Grenadier Guards, adopting the French bearskin caps and grenade badges, the pub followed and became the Grenadier. Officers of the regiment are customers when not on ceremonial duties at the royal palaces nearby.

The delightfully old and very rare pewter bar is central, right in front of you as you come into the pub. The room has a narrow ledge around it to rest your drinks on as space is at a premium in such a small pub, causing many customers to take their drinks outside into the attractive mews. The walls have lots of military history on display, including a collection of Wellington memorabilia. Look out for the painting of a military dinner with separate key to the guests. There is a large sign in the bar recommending the house special, a Bloody Mary, which seems entirely fitting. Customers seek out this historic pub for this reason alone, where the record is having served some 300 in one day. Other quirky features include a notice stating that only people arriving by taxi or on foot will get served.

You will quickly see the masses of bank notes, as dollar bills and other money from around the world are pinned to the ceiling, with messages written on, directed to one officer in particular. A Subaltern in the Foot Guards known simply as "Cedric" is said to have met an untimely demise in the cellar one night in the 1770's whilst playing cards. Apparently Cedric was caught cheating and unable to pay his debts, causing him to be beaten to death by his supposed comrades. Tourists have since taken it upon themselves to decorate the pub this way to help pay off the ill-fated Grenadier's debts, we added bank notes from Egypt, Ghana and Malaysia.

The ghost of Cedric has allegedly been sighted, with the best example, the faint face of a young man, sporting the type of moustache popular in the military at the time, captured in a photo. People have reported hearing a man sighing, and loud footsteps coming from the cellar, where staff have also discovered broken glasses, furniture being moved and even experienced some physical contact. One New Scotland Yard officer claims to have been burned on the hand by an invisible cigarette. A distinct chill in the air and icy blasts have been witnessed, particularly in September during the anniversary of Cedric's death.

Signs in the bar point to the "Wellington Room" and the "Boot Room" within what is still one of London's smallest pubs. The tiny space is decorated with military costumes, paintings and other artefacts with names and dates of battles adorning the walls. These sit alongside newspaper clippings detailing sightings of Cedric, believe these if you will.

The Guinea

Another Mayfair institution, on a site which has had an inn since 1423, with extensive famous clientele with a reputation for American style grills tucked away in an attractive mews.

The pub's website states that there has been an inn on this site from 1423. In 1696 Lord Berkeley sold his home on Piccadilly to the First Duke of Devonshire, who renamed it Devonshire House. Lord Berkeley agreed not to build on the land at the rear of the house, as the Duke was keen to preserve the view from his new home, which we now know as Berkeley Square. Just off the square in a small street called North Bruton Mews, stood what we now know as The Guinea.

There had apparently been a small alehouse on this site called the Pound, referring to a cattle pound or enclosure, for the previous 150 years. This served the workers in what would at the time have been mostly fields in Mayfair. Towards the end of the 17th century fine houses had become established in Mayfair, with a social scene to match, where carriages were housed locally. Many servants, coachmen and stable hands replaced farm labourers as customers, during the period following a re-build in 1741.

In 1755, as guinea coins began to be minted, named after the region of West Africa, the pub was renamed The Guinea. As the value of the coin fluctuated, the government decided to fix it at 21 shillings, or one pound, one shilling. This led to the pub being referred to as "The One Pound, One", although it has never officially changed its name since 1755, despite several incarnations and changes of ownership along the way.

By 1952 North Bruton Mews had been renamed Bruton Place. Rationing was in place from World War II, and large numbers of Americans remained in London. This inspired Alastair Greig, who took over the pub as a tenant, and realised that offering sirloin steak would be a great way of attracting the American servicemen, with deep pockets thanks to their overseas allowances. Greig sourced the finest beef with a simple offering allowing customers to choose the size of their steak before it was cooked.

Tables at The Guinea became highly sought after and the pub has continued to attract celebrities from stage, screen and the world of sport. Regulars included Princess Margaret, Elizabeth Taylor and Richard Burton, Charlton Heston, Frank Sinatra and Jack Nicklaus. It remains popular with American visitors, and is also renowned for hosting property deals in the small restaurant at the rear. They still specialise in grilling the very best beef available in the UK and also serve sustainable fish from British day boats. The menu is complemented by an extensive wine list, designed to ensure a delicious dining experience for everyone.

There is also a fabulously appointed private dining room for special events on the first floor, which can also be re-arranged as a board room, described as atmospheric and decorated with pine panelling. This caters for groups of up to 28 people, and has hosted many great events throughout its long history. Portraits of famous past residents of Mayfair line the walls.

The pub also enjoys a splendid reputation as a pie shop, claiming to serve arguably the best steak and kidney pie in the world. Opposite the pub stands one of the more widely known Italian restaurant chain outlets, which looks out of place in this quiet residential Mayfair mews. Inside the pub, the front bar is small and caters for peak time, standing up trade. The dark wood surfaces and low lighting are designed to create an aura of calm. The menu appearing on beer mats makes for easy reference and no doubt leads to many an impulse pie purchase.

1 Middle Street, Smithfield, EC1A 7JA

Hand & Shears

The plaque outside dates this at 1132, and states that an ale house on this site was famous for hosting an annual cloth fair, now a true local with a host of regulars.

This handsome and ever so slightly battered old pub is tucked away on Middle Street, off Smithfield's main drag, and is known by regulars as the "fist and clippers." It is steeped in history with lots of character. The current pub dates from 1849 and thus has a wealth of original Victorian features with a Grade 2 listing. There has however been an inn on this site since at least the 12th century, although has a sign on the front proudly stating that was established in 1532.

The name comes from the annual cloth fair, which took place in the surrounding streets for 2 weeks, starting on St Bartholomew's Day, 24th August, from 1133 until its inclusion in 1855 as part of the larger Bartholomew Fair. It was traditional for the Lord Mayor of London to open the fair from the steps of the pub, by cutting a symbolic first piece of cloth. It is from this ancient ceremony that today's custom of cutting a piece of ribbon to mark the opening of a shop or other new building derives.

The Cloth Fair was a colourful event which attracted merchants from many countries, who often became unruly, due to the quantity of drink consumed. To settle any disputes that may have arisen, while the cloth merchants were trading, a Court of Piepowder (or piepoudre) was set up in the pub for the duration, establishing the strong link between the pub and the cloth fair.

For some time the pub was allowed to use the insignia on its sign, of the Merchant Taylor's Company, who policed the fair. Anyone who was found to have not upheld the bylaws of the time was "tried" at the pub, often leading to a period in the stocks or a flogging. Today the pub is adorned with the image of a pair of draper's shears slicing through a silken cloth.

More serious crimes resulted in executions taking place outside the nearby Newgate prison, where tradition dictated that the condemned man could have his last drink in this pub. This slightly gruesome practice ceased in 1849, the year the present pub was constructed, and public executions ceased completely in 1868, partly due to campaigning by Charles Dickens.

Entrance to the pub is via a central door, which opens in two circular halves, which you have to squeeze through. Signs on the walls say they are pleased to announce they are Cask Marque inspected, being an official Courage beer supplier and proud to be part of London. At the same time, they politely ask customers to adopt smart dress when visiting the pub. The entrance to the Saloon bar had the letter "S" missing on our last visit although customers appeared to still know where they were going without its help.

The interior is divided into four separate rooms, all served from a central island bar. One of the rooms could be described as a snug, with bare boards, wood panelling and plain décor, referred to as down to earth and not fussy. There are a couple of gas fires plus some interesting prints and old photographs on the walls. There are also many medical themed cartoons on the walls, as a nod to the many surgeons, and other medical staff, from nearby St Bartholomew's Hospital, who frequent the pub. It is open all day, however not at weekends.

Hoop & Grapes

Described as a blissful marriage of charm and tradition, a centuries old pub which has survived demolition attempts, notorious for hosting clandestine wedding ceremonies and now renowned for showing sports.

The very first record for this site states that it is part of medieval property belonging to the Abbot of the Convent of Westminster, who owned the convent garden that is now Covent Garden. In 1529, when King Henry VIII dissolved the monasteries, he took all their land, and either kept it or gave it to his courtiers. This particular parcel of land passed into the hands of Thomas Sackville, the 1st Earl of Dorset, great-nephew of Ann Boleyn and Lord High Treasurer to Queen Elizabeth I. This pub is truly a survivor and dates from 1721, which makes it much older than other celebrated City taverns.

English Heritage noted that it was originally a terraced house, for residential use only by the vintner. If the owner was engaged in business as a wine merchant they, or more likely their descendants, may have been influential in this being converted to a public house in about 1832. The cellars below the building probably date back to the time when the Fleet River was canalised during the period 1670 to 1674.

When Farringdon Road and Farringdon Street were driven through the area between 1840 and 1860 this cleared some of the existing slums and built on top of the River Fleet. The Fleet prison stood on the eastern side of the river, known predominantly as a debtor's prison, until it was demolished in 1864.

The pub became notorious for its Fleet marriages, clandestine ceremonies performed without a marriage license. These took place in the prison chapel and later increasingly, in the surrounding taverns. The Hoop and Grapes became a regular venue. Some 6,000 Fleet marriages took place in one year alone, before they were brought to an end by the passing of the Marriage Act of 1753, which removed the earlier legal "loophole".

The building is tall and narrow, hemmed in on either side by more modern but bland looking office buildings. It was earmarked for demolition in the 1990's, but saved from this fate due to its rich history and heritage. It does tend to look out of place, although lives to tell the tale and is now a Grade 2 listed building.

The name Hoop and Grapes was once quite common for a pub, corrupted from Hop and Grapes, where the sign would feature a garland of hops and a bunch of grapes. Today the hoop part refers to the metal bands used to hold a wooden barrel together, and the grapes refer to wine.

These days the pub is owned and operated by the Kent-based brewery Shepherd Neame, the oldest brewers in the country, with a history that apparently pre-dates their official formation year of 1698. The pub once won a "Perfect Pint" award for exceptional beer-keeping. They also offer many fine wine and whiskies, plus unusual nowadays, a selection of cigars, should you wish to accompany your nightcap in style, although presumably to take outside onto the heated patio and balcony area. This area proves popular throughout the year, with outdoor spaces at a premium in this part of the City, with street signs of famous grounds around the big screen reminding you that the emphasis is regularly on football games.

Back inside, there are traditional pursuits including darts and poker in the games room and live sport. The pub uses the MatchPint application to market their TV listings and sporting events. There is also a pair of fantastic function rooms available for private hire, for special occasions, including modern day weddings in view of the specific history that this pub has in hosting these celebrations.

94 Cowcross Street, Smithfield, EC1M 6BH

The Hope

Smithfield institution retaining local licensing laws allowing it to still serve legendary breakfasts very early in the morning and lots of other history. Opposite the old meat market.

The meat market at Smithfield has existed for some 1,000 years and in present form since the 1860's. This has changed enormously over the years mostly due to food hygiene and general health and safety regulation changes. Many of the traders also blame changes in drink driving laws and the introduction of the London congestion charge, which kicks in at 7 am, for changing the character of the market.

Nowadays the market is seen to be more like a row of butchers' shops, with refrigerated units, rather than an open market. It also operates at more civilised hours. However, some things have remained the same. The "Bummarees", as the porters at Smithfield are known, are still around in their blood-stained, white coats. The Hope is one of only two pubs left in the area that open early, supporting the more traditional operating hours of the market.

The pub was established on this site in the late 18th century, although the current pub dates from the 1870's, where it was likely to have been the work of Isaac and Florence, who were responsible for the construction of several buildings in this area. One of the partners Lewis Henry Isaacs also designed the Farmiloe building close by in St John Street.

This Grade 2 listed building is a popular location for film makers today. The Hope's name probably comes from a corruption of Hoop and Grapes or possibly Hop and Grapes, once common tavern names, denoting that both beer and wine were available. The interior has many surviving late Victorian era tiles and etched glass, indicating significant investment at the time.

It continues to serve the "Full Monty", its legendary full breakfast, best enjoyed with a glass of stout or light ale. The wider menu is said to have resulted from teaming up with Pieminister to provide a selection of award winning pies, made with exceptionally good pastry and delicious, ethically sourced British ingredients. Reflecting the changing time, and even being close to Smithfield meat market, you can also enjoy vegetarian options, and they even have a vegan pie on the menu.

One particular recommendation, suggested if you are visiting for the first time, is to try the "Mothership" if you want a real pie experience. The pie of your choice has a tower of buttery mashed potato, minty mushy peas with gravy on top, then covered in cheese and sprinkled with crispy shallots, one not to be missed.

The menu includes tasty snacks that are perfect with a pint if, for some reason, you don't fancy the full on pie feast. These include a range of patties, free range sausage roll and pork scratchings, described as amazing and seemingly also good value. These can all be washed down in the Juniper Room, which is a dedicated gin parlour on site, where an extensive and varied selection is available.

The pub is now independently run although owned by Ei Group, formerly known as Enterprise Inns plc, who are the largest pub company in the UK, with around 5,000 mostly leased and tenanted pubs. The Hope's own website describes this as being a lively boozer with crafty drinks and tasty food to mop it all up, although, for some reason, says it is Clerkenwell, rather than Smithfield.

St Michael's Alley, Cornhill, EC3V 9DS

Jamaica Wine House

Regarded by some as the essential City pub, the Jamaica Wine House is situated just off busy Cornhill in the much quieter reaches of St Michael's Alley. This is one of the narrow lanes in The City, medieval in origin but which also show what the square mile would have looked like in the 18th and 19th centuries, set within a labyrinth of courts and alleys, in the ward of Cornhill. The character Ebenezer Scrooge from Charles Dickens novels apparently had a counting house nearby.

The pub can trace its origins back to 1652, when Pasque Rosee opened a coffee shop on the site. He was a servant to a merchant called Daniel Edwards, a trader in Turkish goods and also imported coffee. This allowed him to help set Rosee up in business, with the first coffee shop in London, which was visited by the diarist Samuel Pepys as early as 1660. Some accounts state that this was alternatively known as The Turks Head, which seems possible given the trading relationships in place.

By the end of the 17th century there were over 3,000 coffee houses, although the Jamaica Coffee House had become popular as a meeting place for merchants who traded in the West Indies and also Turkey, including in the sugar and slave trades. There is still a plaque on a wall that reads "Here stood the first London coffee house at the sign of the Pasqual Rosee's Head 1652".

As coffee houses began to decline in popularity, it took on its new identity as the Jamaica Wine House in 1869, mainly because the owners at the time, wine merchants E.J. Rose, had a bottling plant in nearby Shoreditch. The pub we see today dates back to 1885. It was designed by architect Banister Fletcher who would go on to write a book on architectural history in 1895 and surely would have been delighted to know that his creation remains such an important local landmark, centuries on.

Now Grade 2 listed and affectionately known as the "Jampot" the pub has no discernible links to the Caribbean, despite its name. It is also very much a pub rather than a wine house, also as its name would suggest. The building went through extensive restoration work in 2009, having been acquired by the brewers Shepherd Neame, who serve their regular offerings such as Spitfire and Whitstable Bay. The interior is dominated, at least at ground floor level, by magnificent and ancient, wooden dividing panels. Beer is definitely the focus of attention in this pub today.

There is a clear split between three distinct sections of the bar, where customers are served separately for each section. Barrels take the place of tables, for the standing customers to rest their drinks. Crowds regularly spill out into the alleys, drinks in hand, especially during hot summer evenings, and it is described as a rather lovely way to drink al fresco.

The restaurant downstairs provides a chance to choose from the extensive wine selection, in the cellar bar called Todd's, which can easily be overlooked. This is a shame as it is an attractive area to relax in, providing somewhere to sit and eat during early evening periods, particularly when the upstairs bar is heaving.

33 Rose Street, Covent Garden, WC2E 9EB

Lamb & Flag

Tucked away down an alley this is a very old pub. Covent Garden was still fields until around 1600 when the 4th Earl of Bedford was given the land by Henry VIII, who had previously seized it from Westminster Abbey, when he became King. This was used originally as the larder for the church, Covent being the Anglo-French term for convent.

The Earl was thinking progressively and wanted to build a more fashionable area on his newly acquired land. He commissioned Inigo Jones, the leading architect of the day, to design an arcaded square to attract wealthy home owners onto his land. The remnants of this Italian style square at Covent Garden are still visible today and have been surrounded since by fine houses.

The pub displays a small, framed summary of its origins, including the fact that the first mention of the site occurred in 1635, when the freehold was sold by the Earl of Bedford. The first known building was constructed in 1638/9 by Captain Thomas Constable of King Street, and was referred to as an alehouse in Rose Street by the poet John Dryden, who lived nearby in Long Acre. This was re-built in 1688 when the passage through the ground floor was made. Another famous resident in the area at the time was the poet Samuel Butler, who lived in Rose Street until his death in 1680. The earliest recorded use of the premises is from 1772 when it was called The Coopers Arms, and the licensee was George Cook.

Dryden was unfortunately attacked by rogues and beaten, as he passed by on his way home late one night, in 1679. The thugs had been hired by a business rival, the 2nd Earl of Rochester. No-one was ever charged for this crime, probably because people feared the Crown's power and there could have been more parties involved, but it was certainly a very well-known incident at the time.

Details of the attack and the reward offered are still visible on a plaque in Lazenby Court, alongside the pub. Dryden was England's first Poet Laureate in 1668. In his honour, the upstairs bar in the pub, accessed via very creaky old stairs, has for some time been known as the Dryden Room.

As the quality of the clientele declined, the pub became known for bare knuckle fights, a common entertainment in many London pubs, while the 'sport' remained legal in the 18th and 19th centuries. It was renamed the Lamb and Flag in 1883. The ancient sign was a popular sight throughout the country, believed to refer to Jesus Christ for the lamb and the dragon slaying St George for the flag.

The contests took place either in the yard in front of the pub, or inside in the back room, which appears hardly changed today. The pub became known locally as "The Bucket of Blood" reflecting the vicious nature of these fights and inevitable outcomes witnessed.

The ground floor has a long, narrow bar with various ornate wooden panels at the front. There is very little natural light, having originally been lit by candlelight and later by gas lamps. Wooden floors, oak beams and brass fittings abound and a lamb and flag appears etched to the right of the bar. There is a slight curiosity in the ground floor gentlemen's toilet: poems handily displayed for reading, copies of which can also be purchased at the bar. Keep an eye out for the picture wall in memory of late regulars.

In the upstairs dining room, the pub proudly states that they are about honest food, well sourced ingredients, and quality cuts of meat. Their team of talented chefs produce consistently delicious dishes, which are very popular with the clientele.

Lamb Tavern

Part of the rich tapestry of the City of London since 1780, situated adjacent to Lloyd's of London, within the covered Leadenhall Market plus more recent movie based history.

This pub was first built in 1309. By the end of the 14th century it was firmly established as a market, and for many years the site of the City granary. Unfortunately the original Leadenhall Market, just off Bishopsgate, was badly damaged in The Great Fire of 1666 and was rebuilt in its present form with a large lead roof, hence the name Leadenhall. However it's not certain it was originally built as a public place. The site itself has even grander origins, appearing as far back as AD 50 and then rebuilt in AD 120 by the Romans, as part of the Basilica, then the largest building of its kind, except for the Basilica Ulpia in Rome itself.

The sign in the current pub states that it was established in 1780, starting as a private house selling real ale, under the stewardship of James Pardy. The current building dates from 1881, when Leadenhall Market was re-built in iron and glass. This was designed by the architect and surveyor Sir Horace Jones, who had also overseen the construction of Smithfield Market, Billingsgate Market and Tower Bridge, although sadly he died before it was finally completed.

The Victorians knew the social importance of the pub, and this is one of the most famous, retaining its Grade 2 listed status. There is elegant and ornate architecture, including the cobble stone flooring, which can be slightly tricky as most drinking is done whilst standing under the market's glass canopy. This was very much how business was conducted for centuries, right back to the establishment of Sir Thomas Gresham's Royal Exchange and then the Stock Exchange, where stock jobbing was recognised as a trade in 1696. Lloyds of London came along in the 1680's on similar lines, with the present Lloyds building standing directly behind the market. This continued to function as a market with the majority of the traders being fishmongers and butchers where, and even today, there remains a butcher in Central Avenue.

After it was purchased by Young's brewery, the pub became famous for selling its own beer to the public and continues to do so up to the present day. The pub's website refers to their continuing partnership with Young's as maintaining an ever-popular hotspot for proper pub grub, carvery and real ale in the hub of the City.

Movie fans may recognise the pub from the film Harry Potter and the Philosopher's Stone, where an optician's shop in Bull's Head Passage was used as the entrance to the leaky cauldron. Some exterior scenes were also filmed here. A fight scene from the 1975 John Wayne film, Brannigan, was shot here. It is also used for wedding receptions and other functions, and has been run by the Morris family for many years.

You actually get two pubs from one, as The Lamb Tavern stands alongside Old Tom's Bar, within the enclosed market. This takes its name from a character that used to live in the market in the early 1800's, which was actually a gander, known to regulars of both pubs. Having escaped from becoming someone's dinner he was adopted by market traders and lived to the venerable age of 37, and is now buried in the market.

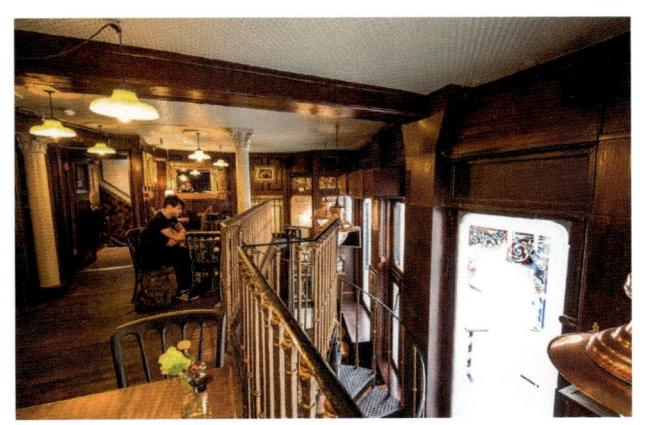

The interior originally included a picture of a smiling Queen Mother pouring a pint of Young's special, with a picture of her grandson Prince Charles above trying to do the same, although apparently with less skill and confidence. These pictures are still on display in the pub today.

Lord Aberconway

> **Unique pub by Liverpool Street station, steeped in railway history and named after the former Chairman of the Metropolitan railway, with elegant mahogany fixtures and numerous pictures.**

Located on Old Broad Street close to, but not actually in Liverpool Street station, described as a stone's throw away, although only if you come out of the station at the end by the McDonalds, in the entrance at the top of the escalators. If you are on Bishopsgate you are unfortunately at the wrong end. The pub is occasionally mistakenly described as a rail station pub with a mezzanine.

The pub is named after Lord Aberconway, the last Chairman of the old Metropolitan railway between 1904 and 1933, when it was amalgamated into the London Transport network. The pub, however, became famous earlier when it was responsible for the opening of the first ever underground railway, anywhere in the world in 1863, which ran from Paddington to Farringdon. There is an elegantly written summary of this on one wall inside, surrounded by historical photographs.

Once extended east to Liverpool Street, where a Metropolitan line station was opened in 1875, the trains run directly underneath, and you can feel the rumbling as trains head to Aldgate East. This is of late Victorian origin and has had various names through the years. It started out as the King and Keys, which records date at 1881, but was later known as both the Refreshment Room and, even as recently as the 1970's, Patmac's Railway Buffet. The pub became known as The Lord Aberconway in the 1980's, where the interior is elegant and traditional in feel, dominated by dark wood. This features various railway memorabilia and the image of Lord Aberconway is portrayed on the sign that hangs outside.

Inside there is still an area described on surrounding walls as "Pac-Man's drinking den", reflecting the earlier claim that it was one of the only bars located directly on the platform, allowing passengers to buy a drink while waiting for their train. An elegant dining area is on the mezzanine level, not obvious from the outside. Also look out for the interesting back bar, with an old clock which appears to still tell the correct time, despite its obvious age.

Underground: Liverpool Street (Central, Circle, Metropolitan and Hammersmith & City Lines)

The pub is at the eastern end of the City, close to The Gherkin and a short walk to Old Spitalfields Market, Brick Lane and into Shoreditch. However, at the time of writing, it is impacted by extensive re-building works taking place to enable the Elizabeth cross rail line to open.

Part of the Nicholson's pub chain, the Lord Aberconway is described as having a quirky vibe. This may be due to the fact that it is, allegedly, haunted by spirits of the victims of The Great Fire of London, as the Monument to this key event stands nearby. The pub markets itself as a pie house, providing cask and craft ales for the modern drinker, pushing through vigorous lunchtime trade of city workers.

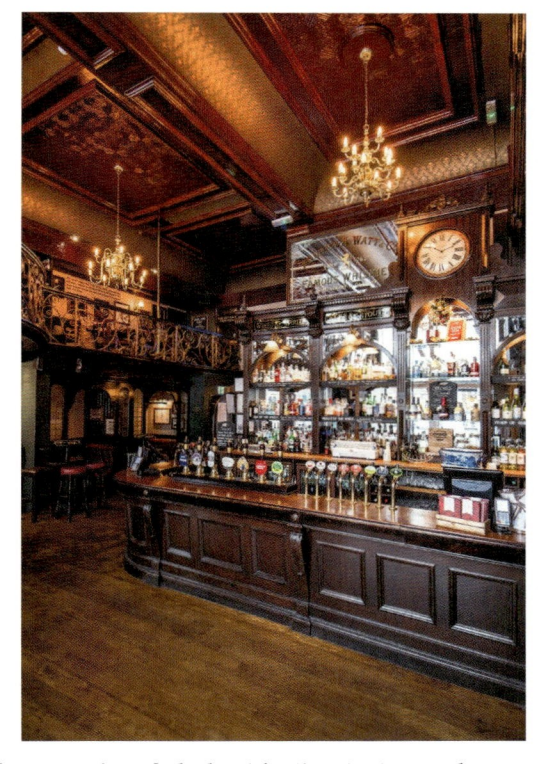

Mahogany furniture sits under warm lamplight. Regal looking tapestries and somewhat faded, old oil paintings adorn the burgundy walls, creating a cosy feel. A mezzanine balcony overlooks the ground floor, with comfortable, cushioned, wood-panelled alcoves beneath. Gold paintwork surrounds the supporting columns, illuminated by grand, old chandeliers and behind the bar a historic hand bell, waits to call out last orders.

The constant flow of customers has no doubt contributed to the worn out floor boards in this extremely popular and well-located pub. The clientele of mainly city workers return time and time again, as part of their daily life and no doubt a visit here makes commuting on crowded trains much more bearable.

61 St Martin Le Grand, St Paul's, EC1A 4ER

Lord Raglan

Lord Raglan was, perhaps unfairly, blamed for the disastrous Charge of the Light Brigade, during the Crimea War, even though this was more likely to have been due to a breakdown in the lines of communications, rather than an order from Lord Raglan himself. There are now various pubs bearing his name, including this imposing example in St Martin's le Grand. This is one of the busiest roads in the City, since the completion of the General Post Office building in 1829, as the majority of coaching traffic from London would start here. Various grand coaching inns would have stood in the vicinity, together with the Bull and Mouth, as this pub was originally known.

The origins of the pub can be found in Elizabethan times when it was known as The Fountain, prior to being destroyed in the Great Fire of 1666. It was rebuilt and became known as The Mourning Bush and then shortened to The Bush. Fragments of the old London wall still stand in part of the pub's cellar. By 1855 it became the Raglan Hotel, in honour of Lord Raglan, one of the key heroes of the Crimean War, who died that year. The name was then subtly changed to become simply The Raglan in the 1950's, finally adopting the name The Lord Raglan in the 1970's.

The pub is located on the historic corner of the City of London's Square Mile, close to St Paul's Cathedral, and looks small from the outside. However, once inside this opens out significantly with a large area extending over different levels. It includes a pool table and an old-fashioned darts board, where can be witnessed many frantic and highly competitive encounters.

The pub is also particularly known for showing the biggest and best live sport, and is refreshingly one of the few pubs in The City that opens on Saturdays and

Sundays. Don't make the mistake though of turning up before they open at 12 pm, in an attempt to get a good seat to watch the game. Ironically, the pub was once allowed to open 24 hours a day by Royal edict, after the landlord opened up to serve King Charles II in the early hours of the morning, on one famous occasion. Sadly this has not been retained, although you would question the need for it in the middle of the night in the City anyway.

Now owned and operated by Greene King brewery, which was established in 1799, the pub's website encourages you to head down to ensure you don't miss the gin of the moment, where an extensive selection of these and other spirits supplement the beers available. In the Summer, this also advertises special events, including most recently a beach party and a Spice Girls party, reflecting another quintessentially English institution.

The pub has an extensive menu and operates as a place to while away an afternoon and evening, watching your favourite sporting events, with good food readily available to refresh you, as well as an extensive drinks range. The food menu is traditional pub fare, although with lighter offerings including toasties, baked potatoes and a range of sandwiches.

Nags Head

> **Dickensian feel and unspoiled interior established in a tiny Belgravia mews building, with a unique collection of penny arcades and other bric-a-brac assembled by a colourful landlord.**

This pub is in a mews, built in 1775 as a row of stables, subsequently housing carriages belonging to wealthy owners of the surrounding grand mansions of the Belgrave estate. London was in the midst of the gin craze in the 18th century, when it was first imported from the Netherlands, and proved to be an instant hit, being both cheap and plentiful. The Gin act of 1751 restricted the sale of gin to fewer premises, which led to the rise in popularity of beer and ale, which was promoted in the 18th and 19th centuries, particularly for its health-giving properties.

The pub would have catered to the drinking needs of staff that looked after the mansions in Belgravia, including those with stables and carriages. The first known occupant of the pub was recorded as a victualler and beer seller, Mr Bunce in 1841, alongside more typical residents including grooms, coachmen and stable-hands. The pub is now in a row converted to smart houses, with ground floor garages.

The current landlord Kevin Moran has developed a reputation as a local character and his name is as prominent, in big letters outside, as that of the pub itself. The pub is very small, possibly one of the smallest in London, where the interior and layout is unlikely to have changed since the 19th century. The back bar would have once been either a courtyard or stables, likely a later addition, and is accessed via a set of narrow stairs to the left of the bar as you enter.

To enable customers of both the front and back bars to be served drinks, the bar is uniquely positioned, split between the two levels. This creates an unusual first impression, if you are not used to it, where customers in the front bar are required to sit on stools which are very low down to enable some form of decent eye contact with the bar staff, who are standing several feet below the bar level. This does, however, allow a close up view of the pub's beer engine, porcelain pump handles, probably the only piece of original Chelsea Pottery still in use in a London pub and over 150 years old. Many of the customers are locals who enjoy the reputation for eccentricity, including an earlier regular, the actor James Mason, who lived locally.

The interior is adorned with many of Kevin's possessions, including military artefacts, plus a collection of antique arcade machines, end of the pier style. There are also saddles, bridles, photos, toys and other bric-a-brac. An old stove from the 1820's adds to the vintage feel with cushioned fireplace fenders, around real log fires. There is even a poster advertising a famous boxing bill at the Albert Hall in 1951, when all three of the Kray brothers were fighting.

This is one of the last links to historical London with a character landlord, established for over 25 years, whose main rules are for customers to hang their coats on one of the pub's many hooks and not to use mobile phones. You can have fun enjoying the interesting objects to view, where the charm and eccentricity of this pub does mean it is well worth an extended visit, particularly to see the huge array of items on display. Keep an eye out for the poster with Dublin pubs which provides a link to our second book.

1-2 Bull Inn Court, Strand, WC2R 0NP

Nell Gwynne

> Traditional, charming and historic pub named after the famous actress tucked away down an alley off the Strand. It has dark wood interior, hanging lamps and a jukebox, with a local feel.

A pub has been on this site since the early 1600's, originally called The Bull Inn, which led to the alley way this is located on, being called Bull Inn Court. This was subsequently renamed after Charles II's infamous mistress, the actress Nell Gwynne, who was born in 1650 and lived a relatively short life to the age of 37. Nell was born and raised nearby at St Martin in the Field and sold fruit in Covent Garden market close by. She was also known to earn a little pocket money with some light prostitution from an early age, before gaining fame as an actress on the Drury Lane stage.

Samuel Pepys described seeing "mighty pretty, witty Nell" on his way to the Strand in 1667. Barnabas Blessed, the Great, Great Grandfather of the actor Brian, was a stationer and bookbinder in the court, at the beginning of the 19th century, and was a well-known regular. In 1897, William Terris, a famous actor of the day, was murdered yards from the pub by a deranged stage hand from the Adelphi Theatre, which is just next door. The pub has retained its interesting history. A previous landlord was an ex-boxer, whose customers included such East End notables as the Kray twins and the Richardsons. For some 20 years after this the publican was an ex-Playboy bunny named Trish.

The pub is now operated by the City Pub Co., who have kept the original exterior look of the building, tucked away as it is down an alley off the hustle and bustle of the Strand. This adds to the welcome, as you have to make an effort to locate this charming and historic little pub, down a gas-lit passageway between Maiden Lane and the Strand, despite being so close to masses of possible passing trade. Look out for the art nouveau tilework in the passage.

They do manage to cram an awful lot into a small cosy space, in just one room, with a set of vertigo-inducing stairs up to the toilets. The room is also very narrow and lacking in natural light, given its layout. However, it is decorated in long-since unavailable, original red Liberty wallpaper, together with subdued lighting with a small raised area at the end of the bar. This also has a much admired and more recently added jukebox, no doubt one of London's best, which is packed with classic old 45 records.

This remains very much a local's pub, many of whom are referred to by name, and all visitors are afforded a generous welcome. The pub offers a great selection of local beers, wines and spirits, and the bar staff even warn you about the Tasty Tipple, being only 2.8% ABV, in case this is too weak for your tastes, although this went down well when I tried it. The pub's website refers to the return of its pickled egg eating challenge, something to look forward to. The pub has also teamed up with their mates at Adnams and Fisher's gin, so they offer an evening of sampling some favorite Suffolk tipples. Occasional celebrities add to the notoriety, appreciating the discretion and anonymity provided, including actor Pierce Brosnan who shot a film close by.

194 Fleet Street, City, EC4A 2LT

Old Bank of England

> Located in the former Bank of England's law courts, with extensive proportions, high ceilings and large artworks, elegant clocks and bank notes on display, celebrating the legend of Sweeney Todd.

This pub benefits from sheer scale, opulence and grandeur and is close to where the cities of Westminster and London meet at the western end of Fleet Street. The present site was formerly two celebrated old inns next to each other, the Haunch of Venison and the original Ye Olde Cock Tavern. Both of these were famous in their own right due to celebrity customers, mostly literary figures.

In 1886 the land was acquired by the Bank of England and both inns were demolished to make way for the law courts branch of the nation's most illustrious banking institution, built in Italian style, which was opened in 1888. Sadly the Haunch of Venison was closed for good although Ye Olde Cock Tavern was re-born and still thrives on the other side of the road.

The new building was designed by Sir Arthur Blomfield and is described as sombre and opulent high Victorian imposing style, and no other pub encapsulates this better. The building operated as the old Law Court's branch of the Bank of England until 1975, when the premises were taken over by a building society initially. The interior is rococo and faux baroque, built around a large island bar with etched glass, spectacular ceiling, ornate hanging lights, and fabulous paintings.

In 1994 the building was acquired by the Fuller's brewery, who spent a significant amount of time and money completing a major re-fit at the time, to enable this to be re-opened a year later as a new pub. This allowed it to maintain its links to the worlds of finance and law, whilst also being close to Covent Garden. The interior is dominated by the large central bar with a clock on the top. A second clock on the back wall, is placed above a large painting that appears to depict a historical court scene, with an odd animal getting in there too. We noticed a couple of wonderful items with various old one pound notes, attractively framed and displayed in a corner of the very back room, against patterned wallpaper.

The pub is now managed by McMullen & Sons Hertfordshire brewery, who recognise that every pub is different, and this one is an excellent example. The pub's website also suggests that every publican is also different, and they offer a range of business arrangements and approaches to running a pub, operating since 1821, which is even shown on mats on the bar.

As an independent, family-run company, Macs lead the way with innovative ways to give talented operators the chance to enter the trade, and claim not to be constrained by corporate decision making, allowing passionate entrepreneurs to realise their ambitions. This ethos is clearly demonstrated in this, obviously one of their flagship establishments, where the stunning and very lavish interior is undoubtedly one of the best of any pub in Central London.

The pub particularly celebrates the legend of Sweeney Todd, known as the Demon Barber of Fleet Street, by claiming that his shop and the tunnels beneath it stood where today's pub sits, next to the pie shop owned by a Mrs Lovett. This was described as a "meat pie emporium" making homemade produce since 1848. Sweeney Todd visited her pie shop, as she was a long-standing admirer. The couple subsequently married, although apparently she eventually became just another of his victims. Earlier victims often became pie fillings, which made the shop very successful, although present claims that "we are very proud of our pies", reflects a more traditional and far less gruesome approach to the preparation of food from their extensive menu.

95 Fleet Street, City, EC4Y 1DH

Old Bell

> **Classic pub, with stained glass frontage, long association with the printing industry and used by Sir Christopher Wren's stone masons in the 17th century, while building a local church.**

This pub enjoys a long and proud history, having existed as a licensed tavern for more than 300 years. It was built by Sir Christopher Wren and used to house his stone masons, when they were rebuilding St Bride's Church after the Great Fire of London, from 1670 to 1684.

Originally the pub could only be reached through an alleyway off Fleet Street, and its location led to a long association with the printing industry. One of the first printing presses operated from the vicinity, as far back as 1500. The pub's location means it is close to a variety of Central London's key tourist attractions including St Paul's Cathedral, The Royal Pump Museum, The Mercer Art Gallery and of course St Bride's Church. It is also only a short stroll from Ludgate Hill, Farringdon Street and City Thameslink railway line making it a convenient venue for commuters as well as tourists.

The Old Bell shares a location with the infamous villain Sweeney Todd, otherwise known as the Demon Barber of Fleet Street. Todd is a fictional character having first appeared as the villain in the Victorian series, The String of Pearls from 1846. This became a staple tale of Victorian melodrama and urban legend, and has been retold many times since, including in the Tony award winning Broadway musical by Stephen Sondheim. Some eminent scholars dispute the fact that Todd is fictional and maintain he is, in fact based on an historical figure who, had he really existed, may well have called this pub his local.

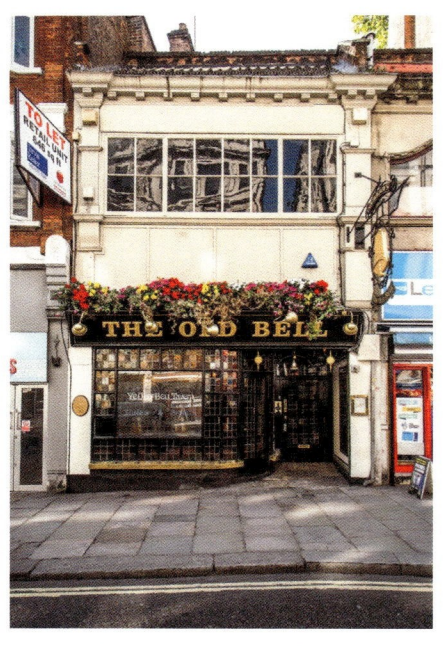

The Fleet Street entrance has a delightful façade with "Ye Olde Bell Tavern Wines & Spirits" written in the stained glass window, where the St. Bride's entrance stands alongside the churchyard. This pub is now one of the Nicholson's chain, reputed for their distinctive buildings, intriguing history and vibrant atmosphere.

The Old Bell is one of many rare gems in the Nicholson's collection, in this case an old gin palace that celebrates being a licenced tavern for over 300 years, now also described on signs outside as a famous pie house. There is an attractive, partially covered alleyway at the back of the pub used for horizontal drinking, and where customers gather in crowds which stretch all the way down St Bride's Avenue and mingle with customers doing the same thing outside the Crown and Sugar Loaf, across the lane - no need for vehicles down here.

Once you step inside, you can immediately sense the unique character of the place. A central bar creates a circular hub, which the interior fixtures radiate out from. The large fireplace provides a cosy touch, in addition to comfortable arm chairs, not seen too often now in central London pubs, where space is often at a premium. There are lots of interesting framed pictures on the walls, including of bells, in keeping with the pub's name, plus maps, announcements from the London Gazette and St Paul's Cathedral, no doubt in view of its close association.

Quality pub food, primarily a range of pies under pastry or mash, is also served, as it should be, with a generous measure of famous British hospitality to complement the drinks. The City of London gin selection is a particular favourite, given that the distillery is just across the road. The pub runs an annual gin festival in the summer, which provides the perfect opportunity to freshen up the drinks menu.

Old Doctor Butlers Head

> Traditional Cask Marque pub, tucked away down an alley in The City, with wooden interior, scarlet curtains and red leather seats, named after a bit of a quack.

For a real feel of what the City of London must have been like in Victorian times, take a stroll down Mason's Avenue, where you will come across this pub, a Dickensian gem of a building. It stands on a narrow thoroughfare, once known as Mason's Alley, which is now a beautiful avenue of half-timbered, narrow old houses. This takes its name from the Mason's Company, which was one of the great livery companies that once had its hall here.

There has been a tavern on this site since 1610, although the original was destroyed in the Great Fire of 1666. The existing building dates back to just after it was re-built. The current pub was re-constructed in Victorian times, with bow windows and the extensive use of dark wood, externally and internally. This was a popular destination for many years for City workers, when it was known as The Old English Divan, and occasionally the Reception Hall. In Edwardian times it was simply known as The German Restaurant, offering steak and kidney puddings, which are still served now. It was then significantly re-modelled in the 1920's.

The original inn was acquired by Doctor William Butler in 1616, who was known as the Doctor of Mirth, and renowned as being a bit of a quack. It now carries his name. His unconventional methods, as a self-proclaimed specialist in nervous disorders, included trying to cure epilepsy through surprising unsuspecting patients, by firing off a pistol shot close to their ears, in the belief it would scare the condition out of them. He was also prone to throwing people in the Thames, or dropping them through a trapdoor, to try to cure them of the plague. He was eventually appointed court physician to James I, which allowed him to obtain an honorary degree in medicine and a more respectable profile, despite his lack of relevant qualifications.

Around the same time, he developed a medicinal ale for gastric ailments, apparently including liquorice and obscure scurvy grass. This was only available from taverns which displayed Doctor Butler's head on their signs. This led to him acquiring a number of ale houses in the capital, of which The Old Doctor Butler's Head is the last one standing. Surprisingly the ale is no longer on the menu, although it is not clear when this was finally withdrawn from sale.

Now regarded as one of the best places to eat in the Moorgate area, also with an attractive outside drinking area down the alley, with barrels to rest on, branded with Shepherd Neame, who re-opened the pub in 2002. The interior is slightly smaller than you expect although attractively laid out with dark wood panelling and leather seating, with four barrels showing favourite brews that are available, separating the bar from the rear seating area.

This is a pub that takes great pride in its food, offering both traditional pub classics in the bar primarily for lunch and innovative, elegant cuisine in their restaurant, thanks to a talented and creative kitchen team, who use seasonal and superbly sourced ingredients across both menus. A function room is also available and BT Sports is on screen. Look out for a couple of amusing framed cartoons of "The Doctor" and beer mats advertising the City of London walk, another Shepherd Neame supported event.

Old Red Lion

> **Established in the 16th century, with links to Oliver Cromwell, and rebuilt in its present form in 1899 retaining its original Victorian character with classic exterior signage.**

This is an imposing pub on the north side of High Holborn, located at the corner with Red Lion Street on this principal main road and thoroughfare, although slightly out of the way for the crowds who come to the West End. It is however still reasonably close to Covent Garden and the British Museum in particular. This was originally established in the 16th century, and was rebuilt in its present form in 1899, retaining its original Victorian character. It appears to have once been known as the "Red Lyon" and regarded as the most important inn in Holborn, as Red Lion Street and Red Lion Square were named after it.

The pub has a particularly attractive exterior sign, with a herald with this most common of pub names and has a key theme displayed on its frontage offering "choice whiskies" to tempt customers inside. Be careful not to trip up on the small step at the front corner entrance, although it is fairly easy to see, displayed in a bold check pattern. Look out for the elegant stained glass windows, with the Greene King fine ales motifs, as they operate the pub.

Legend has it that in 1658 King Charles II had the bodies of Oliver Cromwell and his fellow Roundheads Henry Ireton and John Bradshaw exhumed, to stage a showing and mock execution of their corpses. The bodies were housed overnight in the pub's yard en-route to the gallows at Tyburn. The room upstairs is named the Cromwell Bar to this day in deference to this rather gruesome sounding event.

The brass window ledges on the outside appear very stylish and tempt you inside, where the bare wooden floors are free of clutter, chairs and tables, appealing to customers who like to drink whilst standing. A ledge runs around the perimeter for drinks to be balanced on, where you can sit on stools alongside. There is a glorious and elegant bar, with dark wooden carvings behind a long and rather grand ground floor bar. This has shiny taps and attractive brass fittings, with a particular feature of an 18 inch high statue of the comedians Laurel and Hardy on top of the bar, holding a "welcome" sign, alongside signs for prize winning ales and stouts. Stan Laurel was of course the English half of the famous partnership, although it is not clear if either of the duo set foot in the pub. This may well have happened when they were on tour in the UK in the 1950's, and am sure they would approve of the layout to this day.

Look out for a cartoon style picture celebrating "Henleys Cyder", spelt an usual way although recognising Henley and Sons of Newton Abbott, who were cider makers up to 1927 according to National Archives. Another sign, just next to the steps down to the gentlemen's toilet, advertises Irving golf club, clearly a long way from this location. This can be quieter than other pubs in more popular areas at lunchtimes, although the service more than compensates, allowing for calm relaxation and reflection. Evenings are much busier with brisk trade with workers from the area plus the many locals who frequent it, often standing outside and enjoying their drinks watching the world go by on this most historic of thoroughfares.

Princess Louise

> Original Victorian style, authentic gin palace, with elaborate interior around long island style central bar with extensive use of ornate mirrors and polished dark wood throughout.

This is a Grade 2 listed pub which first opened at the height of the British Empire in 1872 and named after the Princess Louise, the sixth child of Queen Victoria and Prince Albert. Princess Louise was described as fashionable and a talented artist and sculptor, clearly deserving of having a famous pub named after her.

There has been an immense amount of craftsmanship and expense lavished on this pub, especially inside. Standing proud on High Holborn the exterior only provides a brief hint of the truly opulent interior, although does display its name prominently in gold lettering on a black background.

The pub was re-modelled in 1891 and then benefitted from a far more sympathetic rework in 2007, after being closed for 9 months whilst building works were completed. This restored the interior to be more like the original, recreating the layout of corridors and various sized rooms, with glass-sided cubicles that were so popular in Victorian times. The pub is now quite deservedly referred to as a "National Treasure", an accolade Princess Louise would certainly have approved of.

The pub was adopted by Samuel Smiths brewery, who now serve a range of their beers with pub food. Being located near to the British Museum and the University of London, it is frequented by academics, who happily mix with the numerous tourists who seek out the pub for its atmosphere and charm. There is a sign stating that it is a mobile, tablet and laptop free zone, although this is not generally enforced.

The Princess Louise was joint winner, in the best refurbishment class, of the 2008 Pub Design Awards, given annually by CAMRA. Author Peter Haydon included this in his book "The Best Pubs in London" rating it Number 5 in the capital, saying it had "possibly the best preserved Victorian pub interior in London". The pub is also notable for having been the venue for a number of influential folk clubs run by Ewan MacColl and others, helping with the revival of British folk music from the late 1950's.

Allow plenty of time to appreciate the late Victorian décor which is intact in almost every detail. There are lots of ornate mirrors of course, which are even signed by the proud manufacturers, R. Morris Ltd of 293 Kennington Road. There are tiles and glass panels with a mosaic floor and an elaborate ceiling, which is decorated in rich lincrusta, showing that the pub was once sub-divided, with a narrow corridor along the side. There are other similar examples of this layout in Victorian era gin palaces.

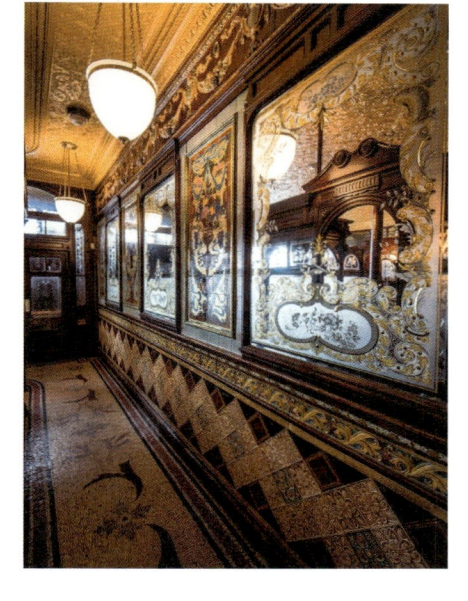

The extensive, island style bar has cast iron, marble effect, columns with golden Corinthian capitals with a central arch made of polished dark wood and topped with a clock and finials. This means the bar staff have to be fit to run up and down to serve customers in the panelled and carved mahogany partitions. Apparently even the gentlemen's toilets are Grade 2 listed, due to their historical and architectural interest, as designed by J. Tyler & Sons, with marble urinals and original tiles.

In addition to the booths there are several larger spaces, including pleasant rooms at both the front and rear, with an attractive skylight. There is a stained glass window at the rear with a music theme, surrounded by floral and fruit displays. This leads to the slightly less ornate dining room upstairs, although this does have a display of pictures of Princess Louise on the walls, and plans in frames up the stairs.

Punch Tavern

> **Dark oak panelling and highly ornate period decor in traditional Victorian venue entered through a very narrow entrance area, with close links to the satirical magazine Punch.**

From a design point of view, this is one of London's most dazzling pubs. There is no frontage as such, entrance is via a long lobby, decorated with mosaic floor, cut glass mirrors and sumptuous glazed tile work, offering a glimpse of what the interior might reveal.

Inside, a huge vaulted skylight allows natural light to pour in. Giant mirrors line one wall and almost everywhere you look, ornate painted panels depict Mr Punch and also Judy. The bar itself is of sturdy Victorian origin, topped in pink marble. All in all a most striking and very welcoming environment, echoing the gin palace boom of the late 19th century.

For many years the pub was called The Crown and Sugar Loaf, an amalgam of two previously separate pubs that joined together. In 1841 the satirical magazine Punch was founded here and the editorial staff then proceeded to make it their pub of choice. During the 1880's the pub changed its name to reflect this and has retained it ever since, even when Punch folded in May 2002, having been previously rescued by the former Harrods proprietor Mohammed Al Fayed.

The current Punch Tavern was re-built between 1894 and 1897 by the Architects Saville and Martin, for the famously big spending Baker Brothers, London's most extravagant and flashy pub entrepreneurs of the late Victorian era. The Punch went on to become one of Fleet Street's most famous taverns, a home from home for generations of newspaper writers and printers. Its famous interior survived both World Wars and the changes arising when newspapers moved out of Fleet Street in the 1980's.

The pub's ownership became complicated, as two thirds was owned by Bass and the remainder by Samuel Smiths brewery. Sometime in the 1990s, when a dispute between the two arose, the pub was effectively split into two, with Bass continuing to run the larger portion with its entrance still on Fleet Street. The other part closed down, until 2004, following an expensive face lift, re-establishing The Crown and Sugar Loaf name. The Punch Tavern was previously managed by the co-incidentally eponymous Punch Taverns, although is now independently owned and a Grade 2 listed building.

The most recent refurbishment has retained the attractive interior from the Victorian and Edwardian eras, demonstrating its period charm. This starts with the glazed and tiled lobby through to the ornate plasterwork, etched glass and bevelled mirrors plus art deco lighting across the main bar area and dining room to the rear.

At the bar you will find a gin and whisky lover's paradise plus an excellent selection of craft beer and cask ales, with a carefully curated wine list. The menu shows a focus on seasonality, including what are described as the finest Sunday roasts in the City. The restaurant style service, in what is essentially still an open bar area, is most welcome. Dogs are treated with as much courtesy as their owners, which is obviously appreciated by visitors, with or without their pets. It is specifically detailed on their website as being a family friendly pub, with an easy to use reservation system, and will happily provide water for the pooch.

Queen's Larder

> Small, wood panelled, 18th century pub with stripped floors, extensive history detailed on plaque on the outside, including being used to store food for mad King George III.

There is an attractive exterior sign detailing the history of the pub, probably the best presented we have seen and prominently displayed at the front. This highlights that the earliest official reference to the tavern, now known as The Queen's Larder, is contained in the deed drawn up in 1710, when Sir Nathaniel Curzon let the house to a London Stationer named Matthew Allam. The mortgage was transferred during the following year to Oliver Humphries and later to a carpenter named Kendrick. The present tavern was then a humble alehouse without an inn sign.

The sign continues that it was during the era that the reigning sovereign, George the III, began to be affected by mental illness and, for a while, he discreetly stayed in Queens Square under the care of Dr Willis. The doctor's treatment which was temporarily successful was helped by the King's consort, Queen Charlotte, who rented a small underground cellar beneath the present tavern in which she stored special delicacies for her sick husband, to relieve the tedium of his confinement.

Queen's Square is actually named after Queen Anne, who died in 1712 mid way through the construction of the square. When the alehouse became a tavern, much later in King George's reign, it was named The Queen's Larder in Charlotte's honour, once the facts became public knowledge.

The Queen's Larder stands in a neighbourhood that is famous for medicine, hospitals and philanthropy. The Foundling Hospital was next to the square in Guildford Street, founded in 1742. Writing of the area R.L. Stevenson once observed that it seemed to have been set aside for the "humilities of life and the alleviation of all hard destinies". There is now a statue of Queen Charlotte in Queens Square and Great Ormond Street Hospital is also close by.

The pub stands on a passageway, Cosmo Place, which is never particularly crowded and actually encourages everyone to sit outside on the benches provided. It also caters for pets. This can therefore be an excellent spot to sip a drink, whilst watching the world go by. It is away from the main thoroughfare with very light traffic, which makes it hard to believe you are still in residential Central London. This compensates for the interior of the pub, which is small, pleasant and very intimate and it is surprising to know that it is owned and operated by Greene King, who ensure it doesn't resemble being part of a large chain. There is extra seating available in a lounge upstairs if required.

The staff of the pub offer a warm welcome to customers, whether they are regulars from the local community, including employees from nearby Great Ormond Street Hospital, and offices in the surrounding area. Tourists, who manage to find the pub, are invited to stand on the business side of the small bar and have their photos taken pulling a pint for instance, in this traditional and historic English public house. No doubt the photos soon find their way onto social media and many a tourist's photo collection, as a great souvenir of their visit to London.

The pub's own website describes itself as "the cosiest place to have a pint in the wider neighbourhood" allowing you to enjoy the subtle jazz, clown and theatre themes on display, whether you are inside or out, weather permitting. Amusingly the photo of the exterior of the pub appears to have been taken straight after a pretty heavy snowstorm.

48 Parliament Street, Westminster, SW1A 2NH

Red Lion

Politicians' pub in Westminster, with long bar, elaborate ceiling, numerous portraits and illustrious former clientele which includes former Prime Ministers from being directly opposite Downing Street.

This pub stands on the site of a medieval tavern, known in 1434 as the Hopping House. The tavern then passed through various hands, taking a variety of names in its early years, before being bought by the Crown in 1531. Perhaps due to the age of the pub, the long and narrow building appears slightly lop-sided as it stands on its corner site. It was designed by the architectural team of William Kent, Sir John Soane and Sir Charles Barry, and completed in 1845.

A young Charles Dickens became a regular visitor, noting that the pub's landlady was a kind hearted soul, whose attitude to him was "admiring as well as compassionate". This no doubt inspired him to use the pub as the inn where David Copperfield asked for "a glass of genuine stunning ale" and was given this with a kiss from the bar maid who served him. As a token of gratitude, the pub prominently displays a bust of Dickens on one of its walls. Geoffrey Chaucer also has a bust honouring him, although it is not possible that he ever drank here, having died in 1400.

Many of the customers will remember the now retired landlord, Raoul De Vere, a former policeman who pioneered the Pub Watch scheme. This involved close co-operation with police forces and allowed him to become influential with law makers as the scheme became more widely adopted. Standing so close to Downing Street and the Houses of Parliament, the pub became a popular haunt for Prime Ministers serving all up until Edward Heath in the 1970's, and including the likes of Sir Winston Churchill and Clement Atlee. In those days you could stroll over the road, relatively unchallenged right up to the door of 10 Downing Street.

A constant stream of tourists now passes through this Fullers owned and operated pub, mingling with a large group of long-standing regulars. These include those looking for refreshment having contributed to the business of government in the Palace of Westminster, or Her Majesty's Treasury, both of them but a short walk away. The pub is also a couple of doors away from the former residence of Sir George Burke, a close associate of Isambard Kingdom Brunel. Being an industrious type Brunel apparently rigged up a mechanism involving a bell and a length of string to summon his friend Sir George to the window to pick up messages, often inviting him for a walk or a beverage.

Inside, the bar is positioned along one wall, extending to under the stairs, which lead to the upstairs dining room. The room is lined with wood panelling and displays of glorious grandeur from Victorian times. This area became famous in the early 1990's as the meeting place for Labour party modernisers, who developed the principles of New Labour. Pictures on the walls, as expected, are mostly of political figures, and this is likely to be the best place in the city for lovers of political history to explore. It is used regularly by Foreign Office staff and MP's plus Metropolitan police officers, who used to be based in nearby Scotland Yard.

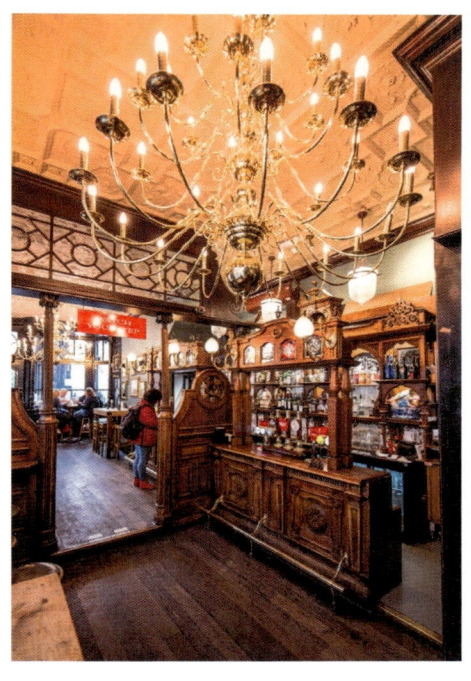

The recent refurbishment has further enhanced the interior with the clubby cellar bar now called The Cabinet Room, and decorated in the style of an old gin bar. Look out for the chandeliers and moulded ceilings. There is also has some outside bench seating, where you can consume Fullers traditional beers, or select from a good range of wines and food, which is also available on each of the three grand floors. The pub's website has an attractive feature, presenting a 360-degree tour online, navigating right through the pub.

2 Duke of York Street, Mayfair, SW1Y 6JP

Red Lion

Victorian former gin palace in Mayfair with all original features including etched glass panelling, renowned for being one of the most photographed pub interiors in London.

This pub is regarded as a survivor having been nearly wiped out in the Blitz, plus also cleverly avoiding redevelopment initiatives as well as earlier slum clearance works. There has been a pub on this site called The Red Lion since 1788. The present pub was built with its classically Georgian façade in 1821, remaining on the same site as the earlier pub, as was a common practice in the late 18th and early 19th centuries. This was then remodelled in the Victorian era, in the 1870's, resulting in the varying styles of glasswork and ornate Victoriana at its finest, with hand carved mahogany decor. This could be described as a typically elaborate Victorian gin palace and is undoubtedly an excellent example of which there are various in Central London.

This Grade 2 listed pub has no doubt always been busy, given its location close to the clubs and grand houses of the area of St James', although it is small with little room available for seating inside. Fortnum and Mason is nearby, together with the shops of Jermyn Street and Piccadilly, so it provides an excellent resting place for weary shoppers, if you can get a seat. If not, outside seating is provided on the pavement, which is not as dangerous as one might think as it occupies a spot on a relatively quiet road, ideal for street side socialising and watching the world go by.

This pub could well have the most photographed interior in London, due to its fantastic decorations and ornate mirrors. These were crafted by Walter Gibb and Sons of Blackfriars, using some of the most advanced etching techniques available at the time. They cover pretty much every available wall, including the recently developed and very ornate etching and engraved decorations. The mirrors are ornate and embossed with silver fittings which attractively offset the generally dark wood background. This is exaggerated by having a number of empty glasses kept on top of the dark wooden bar, which provides the impression of there being even more glassware on display.

One theory is that the mirrors were deliberately commissioned by a local magistrate to reduce the privacy available in the snugs and the likelihood of casual prostitution taking place, all somewhat contrary to the more general approach of the time. None of this matters of course when it was voted "Most Authentic Pub 1999" by CAMRA, a rare and much appreciated accolade.

Now owned and operated by Fullers brewery, which offer an excellent feature on their websites, a gallery of 360 degree images of their pubs and this is a particularly excellent one. This pub has always recognised the importance of great tasting food and expertly stored drink, plus they serve a variety of bar snacks and traditional pub food and can cater for private parties on request. The small and slightly cramped interior means that a lot of drinking takes place on the street outside, with the small entrance doors at each side taking some considerable hammer with people constantly passing drinks in and out.

90 Saint Martin's Lane, Leicester Square, WC2N 4AP

The Salisbury

> Classic Victorian pub on striking corner site in the heart of theatre land, former prize fighting venue, with original etched glass and carved mahogany, also used as a film location.

This pub was built as part of a six storey block in about 1899 on the site of an earlier pub, which had been known under several names, including the Coach and Horses and Ben Caunt's Head, after a landlord who was also a bare knuckle fighter, known as the Nottinghamshire Giant. This established the pub as venue for such sporting activities, which were popular in the early 19th century.

A new lease was taken out in 1892 by the Marquis of Salisbury, a direct descendant of Robert Cecil, the First Earl of Salisbury. Each of these men were favourites of the Queens of their times, Victoria and Elizabeth I respectively. The Marquis in particular was a great supporter of the public house, resisting moves to reduce the number to try to cut down on the levels of drunkenness seen in the capital.

The pub was probably a wine merchants as well as a gin palace, given it was known as the Salisbury Stores. It also became somewhat of a haven for the theatrical gay community from Oscar Wilde's time, when there were low levels of tolerance, not to mention the fact that homosexuality was still a criminal offence. The Stores part of the name was dropped in the 1960's as it increasingly became known as a pub for actors, including many who were performing in the theatres close by.

The Salisbury was used as a location, both inside and out, for the 1961 suspense film The Victim, starring Dirk Bogarde and Sylvia Syms. Other films featuring the pub were Travels with My Aunt starring Maggie Smith and more recently The Boat that Rocked, starring Philip Seymour Hoffman. In view of its position in the heart of theatre land, generally described as being in Covent Garden, the pub is a popular place for refreshments before and after theatre performances. The sign over one bar pointing the way to the "stage door" actually points the wrong way, as The Noel Coward Theatre next door is on the other side of the pub.

Now Grade 2 listed, the pub is named after Lord Salisbury, who was British Prime Minister three times between 1885 and 1902. The Cecil family's coat of arms lies between two angels supporting a canopy above the door on the corner. Cecil Court, nearby, is also named after the family.

The serial killer Dennis Nilsen attempted to murder Andrew Ho, a student from Hong Kong in 1979, after meeting in The Salisbury. Although Ho went to the police and Nilsen was questioned, the student chose not to testify, so no charges were brought against Nilsen, who tragically went on to murder fourteen young men.

This is now a most striking Victorian pub with an elegant bar, surrounded by etched and polished glass mirrors, fine upholstery and carved woodwork, following a refurbishment in 1963 to return it to its original glory. The interior is recognised on CAMRA's national inventory as being "an historic pub of national importance". The "SS" motif etched into the glass relates to the pub originally being called the "Salisbury Stores". Other fittings include art nouveau bronze nymphs, holding long-stemmed flowers with light bulbs in the middle, which are said to be original. Look out for the window broken in the Poll Tax riots.

The speciality of the house is the daily roast, together with other traditional English pub fayre dishes. There are many things about this pub which are reassuring and consistent, not least the very pleasant and helpful staff. You have the feeling that the staff and management are glad to see you, to welcome new faces and the return of many old friends.

Sherlock Holmes

> Traditional style pub with Sherlock Holmes themed memorabilia, including a fully stocked replica of his flat at 221b Baker Street, plus restaurant, attractive roof garden and merchandising area.

This pub is a Victorian era themed pub near Charing Cross station and Trafalgar Square. It was originally a small hotel called the Northumberland Arms, when it was first opened in the 1880's, given its location on Northumberland Street. It was also known as The Northumberland Arms when it became a more traditional tavern. The traditional façade has gold lettering and hanging baskets.

The association with the fictional detective Sherlock Holmes arose when The Northumberland Arms appeared in the 1892 story The Adventures of the Noble Bachelor, written by Sir Arthur Conan Doyle. Holmes and his trusted assistant, Dr Watson, used to frequent a Turkish bath, which in the stories was located right beside it at 25 Northumberland Street. The entrance to the women's Turkish bath can still be seen in Craven Passage at the rear of the men's baths. Various Holmes' fans maintain that the present pub was also featured in the most famous of Conan Doyle's Holmes novels The Hound of the Baskervilles, published in 1901.

The pub was then refurbished and reopened under its present name in December 1957. Its owners at the time, Whitbread and Co, were fortunate in being able to purchase the entire Festival of Britain Sherlock Holmes exhibit, once it had returned from a world tour, including going to New York where it was displayed at the Plaza Galleries. Marylebone Public Library, with the support of the Abbey National, which had its headquarters on the site of 221b Baker Street, decided to create an exhibition based on the fictional detective, in its own permanent home in a themed pub in Central London, where it would appeal to Holmes' enthusiasts visiting from around the world. The pub was restored to its late Victorian form and the main exhibit, a detailed replica of the study in Holmes' fictional apartment at 221b Baker Street, was installed on the upstairs floor.

This can be viewed from behind a plate glass wall from the first floor, Holmes themed restaurant, as well as from the roof garden and through small windows in the upstairs hallway. Supporting displays in the bars include theatre posters, Dr Watson's old service revolver, political cartoons and the stuffed head of the Hound of the Baskervilles, which is prominently mounted.

Four Holmes enthusiasts, with the full support of the family of Sir Arthur Conan Doyle, designed and planned the exhibition, collecting materials for display, including a Persian slipper to hold Holmes's tobacco, a jack-knife for Holmes to pin his unanswered correspondence to the mantelpiece with, and a gasogene for Dr Watson's soda. You will also see artwork and props from the many stage and screen adaptations of the story, including the famous pipe, violin and scientific equipment. Each day crumpets were supplied by a local baker and these were left on a plate in the sitting room with two different sets of bite marks.

Over the years, the exhibits in the downstairs bar areas have been augmented with photographs of the actors, who have played Holmes and Watson since the original display was set up. The collection is curated and maintained by the Sherlock Holmes Society of London.

Today the pub is owned and operated by the Green King brewery, who are based in Bury St Edmunds, who have established a small area at one end of the bar for themed merchandise sales, including Union Jack flags. They also serve Sherlock House Ale and Watson's Golden Ale, extending the themes, all allowing you to be temporarily transported back to Conan Doyle's Victorian London.

1-3 Craven Passage, Strand, WC2N 5PH

Ship & Shovell

> May well be unique as two separate buildings facing each other on the opposite sides of the street, only connected underground by a shared cellar and kitchen.

The pub is located just behind Charing Cross Road station and the Embankment, although its existence is something of a secret for any passing trade close by. It was named after Sir Cloudesley Shovell, who had a distinguished naval career in the 17th century, having risen to earn a commission after joining at the age of 13. Prior to being appointed Admiral of the Fleet he lived in nearby May Place.

Having sustained some great victories, including the capture of Gibraltar, he did, however, gain a reputation for being on vessels that sank. He survived the sinking of his flagship HMS Association, in a naval disaster off the shores of the Scilly Isles at Porthellick Cove in 1707, only to be strangled by a local woman intent on stealing his valuable emerald ring. Shovell's portrait still features on the sign hanging outside the pub, which is divided into two parts facing each other on opposite sides of a small passage-way.

The pub was originally established in the 1730's although the building directly opposite became derelict between 1981 and 1996. The owners of the existing pub became tired of the view opposite and subsequently acquired the property. They connected the two buildings beneath the pavement of Crown Passage and re-opened it as two separate halves of the same pub in 1999, linked only by a tunnel which also contains the kitchen and cellar. This provides a unique offering, full of charm and character for customers, who can choose to sit in one or the other of the sides.

Both buildings are managed by Badger Brewery, owned by Hall and Woodhouse, who started brewing beer in 1777, when Charles Hall set up a brewery in Ansty in Dorset. His son Robert made his nephew Edward

Woodhouse a partner some 60 years later. Hall & Woodhouse now have a number of pubs located across Great Britain, offering their own range of Badger Beers, only sold in their pubs, so they can guarantee the very best quality cask and bottled ales, brewed right in the heart of the Dorset countryside. One of their brews was named after an incident when their head brewer, John Woodhouse, was in the midst of asking his team to sample one of their latest brews. When he got up to leave the room he stumbled briefly as his leg had got tangled up in his pet dogs' lead, so the brew was duly named "Tanglefoot".

The pub's website describes this as being just a stone's throw from Charing Cross station, Buckingham Palace and Trafalgar Square, as well as within walking distance of Covent Garden with its rich mixture of theatres, shops and restaurants. The Ship and Shovell provides the ideal watering hole for a day out in and around the West End and also an ideal venue for a lunch time or after-work do. The smaller of the two bars is furnished with wooden alcoves and is generally quieter than the main bar opposite.

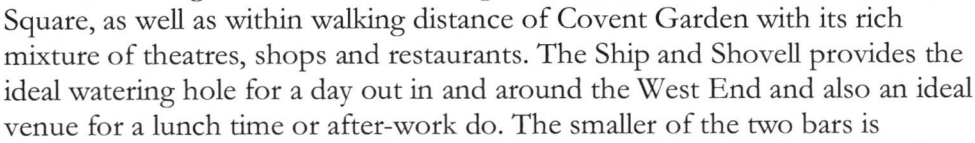

The pub has been welcoming businesses, as well as friends and family to celebrate life's important occasions for many years and you are likely to be in safe hands if you decide to choose this. They encourage getting in touch to host an office party, leaving do, retirement bash or reunion, or indeed to just celebrate a birthday or anniversary. The pub markets selections of sharing platters from their main menu, or separate buffet options, and a booking area can be reserved in the south side of the pub.

12 Gate Street, Holborn, WC2A 3HP

Ship Tavern

> **Mahogany panelled 16th century pub with a rich and vibrant history involving hosting religious ceremonies away from the authorities, with traditional real ale bar and elegant dining area.**

This pub was probably built in the mid-16th century, and the pub's website refers to is as being part of the Holborn scene since 1549. There is an exterior sign that states it was established in 1799, possibly with a different name. This stands on a narrow footpath known as Little Turnstile, where it meets Gare Street. This over-looked a rough area of land known as Lincoln's Inn Fields when first built. Workers from these fields would have been its earliest customers, although the area would surely not have been as tranquil as it now is. Gate Street was named because it supported a large gate, to prevent the livestock and horses grazing on those fields from escaping.

The pub was originally known as a refuge for Catholics when Mary, Henry VIII's daughter, was keen to restore links with Rome. She managed to re-impose Roman Catholic values, although she became deeply un-popular by doing so. Elizabeth I, who succeeded her, was Protestant, and soon Catholics were seeking out the relative safety of The Ship, discreetly arranging for mass to be held in the tavern, instead of being served drinks.

The building was originally timber built within a massive oak frame, which allowed builders to construct false walls, secret rooms and passages. These were used for smuggling, although through religious persecution became known as "priest holes". As the pub was approachable from four directions, lookouts could be positioned to enable a secret mass to be aborted and the premises quickly restored to that of a simple tavern at the first sign of authority. On one occasion when the lookouts were apparently asleep, the military arrived un-announced and killed the priest who was trying to escape. Apparently, his screams can still be heard on "dark and stormy nights".

The pub subsequently became a Masonic lodge in 1736, having been used for meetings for many years before. The pub was also instrumental in creating porter, paying homage to the men who fetched and carried the brew previously known as "three threads". The Fellowship of Porters mainly carried measurable commodities such as grain and foodstuffs, un-loading ships by hand, quickly working up a thirst as a result. An initiation ceremony arose, where porters were expected to drink at least two pots of ale, now four pints, and were paid for their labours, minus the cost of the pots.

The present pub was built on the site of the original tavern in the 1920's and subsequently enlarged, extending the survival of the original pub for over 300 years. The interior has mahogany walls, illuminated by attractive candlelight and a flickering open fireplace. The pub offers great British pub classics as well as daily specials from market suppliers. These are paired with quaffable real ales and a wide variety of over 60 gins from around the globe, many of which are brewed in nearby Holborn. Keep an eye out for their gin of the week, from the full gin list.

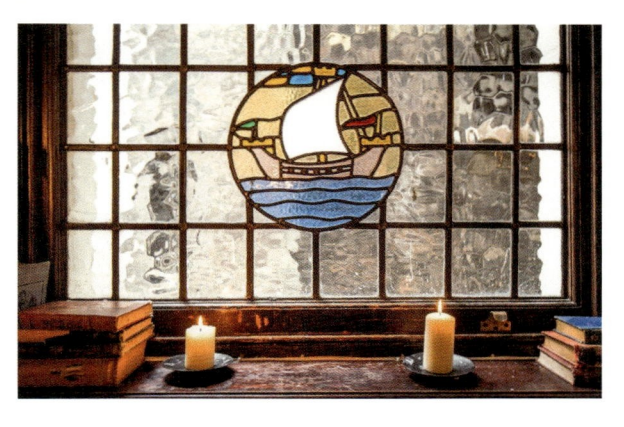

The first floor Oak dining room is full of Dickensian warmth and charm, with elegant wooden panelling and soft lighting, described as a tranquil place to relax. Look out for the clocks of the world from the Bristol Shipping Co. although they appear to have long since stopped working. The pub opens on a Sunday, which is most unusual in this part of the City, where customers are tempted to relax with gin and jazz after feasting from the sumptuous Sunday lunch menu.

Star Tavern

> **Elegant pub in mews location with bookcases, open fireplaces and chandeliers, famous for its notorious 1960's show business and criminal clientele, including the Great Train Robbery gang.**

Established in 1846, Grade 2 listed, and located on a mews street in an area that mostly houses embassies and similar establishments, rather than traditional residential properties. It is close to Belgrave Square, established in 1826 when the Earl of Grosvenor obtained an Act of Parliament allowing him to build there.

The pub was a favourite hangout of movies stars, including Albert Finney, Peter O'Toole and Diana Dors, and other wealthy celebrities of the 1950's and 1960's. It was also renowned for hosting London's inner circle of master criminals, who regularly quaffed its most expensive champagne. This is where most of the planning took place for what was the century's biggest heist, the Great Train Robbery, which netted its 18 man gang £2.8 million, over £40 million in today's money.

After a tip-off from a bent solicitor's clerk, who had somehow become aware that up to £6 million was going to be on a Glasgow to London mail train on 8th August 1963, Bruce Reynolds, an already successful robber, contacted Buster Edwards who was part of the "South Coast Raiders" train robbing gang. This quickly led to a plan being formulated, which Reynolds co-ordinated, regularly driving his Aston Martin from his home in Streatham to meet Edwards and one or two of the other gang members in the Star Tavern, to go over the plan.

Reynolds felt that he had broken in to the upper echelons of the criminal fraternity, after meeting several of the gentlemen robbers of the time here. One party even claimed to have stolen jewellery worth £200,000 from Sophia Loren, bragging about it and even producing a huge roll of banknotes as if to prove their success.

The landlord during this period was a larger than life Irishman called Paddy Kennedy, who swore at his customers, regardless of who they were. Apparently the "posh drinkers" found it entertaining to be hanging around with known criminals and being sworn at by a landlord, with no apparent regard for wealth or status, and who often singled out customers for abuse over a whole evening, to the amusement of everyone else.

Reynolds fled to Mexico after the robbery to live a playboy lifestyle and spend his share of the loot, before returning to the United Kingdom. He was eventually caught with the rest of the gang and sentenced to 25 years in prison, although eventually serving only 10.

Inside the pub, there is plenty of wood panelling and several very detailed chandeliers, with branded mirrors, signs and plaques throughout. The right side of the pub has the bar, where regulars now congregate, with the other side on the left as you enter, opening out into a longer room, divided by an arch. There are old-style, solid fuel fireplaces on both sides.

The dining room on the first floor resembles a library, lovingly preserved with rare and individual beauty. An inevitable snigger will arise if you spot the Thomas Crapper wash basins in the gentlemen's toilets, although Thomas Crapper goes back further than the slang word crap.

Now a Fullers brewery pub, it still requires newcomers to seek directions or be guided by concierges of the local hotels in the area, because it is unlikely anyone will come across it otherwise. This now has a far friendlier clientele and has recently been voted the best historical pub in Central London by the Telegraph newspaper. The pub's website has an excellent 360-degree tour facility and is recognised as one of the best pubs in Belgravia, with emphasis on great service, beers and home cooked food, in comfortable surroundings.

The Swan

> **Bustling Edwardian establishment right opposite Hyde Park with historical links to famous highwaymen, also notorious for creating well known phrases, and now a renowned gastro pub.**

According to records, this pub was established in 1721, being the first date entered in the licensed victuallers register, although widely believed to have been an inn for much longer. This is situated on the old Roman road from London to Exeter, likely a busy coaching inn before this called The Saracen's Head. The pub stood alongside a small ford on the Bayswater stream and, as a result, became a favourite stopping place for coaches to water horses, eat and drink. In the 18th and early 19th centuries the Physic Gardens that lay directly alongside the inn was famous for medicinal remedies attracting customers from far and wide.

The pub's location meant it played a role in history beyond being a simple coaching inn. It was the last pub on the approach to the Gibbet at Tyburn gallows, where the wagons that were taking condemned prisoners to their executions would stop here briefly, so they could have one final drink. The most famous of these was the gentleman highwayman Claude Duval, who had been extremely active on the London to Uxbridge Road.

Executions had been taking place at Tyburn, on the site we now know as Marble Ach, for over 500 years, where the infamous Tyburn tree was erected for mass executions. We know that Duval was born in Normandy in 1643 into a privileged background, so one can only wonder why he chose highway robbery as a career, to be found guilty and sentenced to hang when his luck ran out. His reputation was established through wearing only the finest clothes with some Gallic charm and allegedly never using violence during the robbery of coaches.

One famous example tells of how Duval held up a wealthy businessman travelling with his young and beautiful wife. Apparently, Duval agreed to only relieve the businessman of part of the purse he was carrying, if his wife would do him the honour of dancing a courante, which was a fashionable dance of the time. This was well reported and added to Duval's notoriety at the time, where several pleas for clemency were un-successfully entered on his behalf when captured, as he had not used violence. He had his last drink here on 21st January 1670, after travelling in a caged wagon drawn by a single horse.

This story led to two connected expressions, as the story goes, that the driver of the wagon carrying Duval to his execution asked the landlord to give him "one for the road", meaning the road to the Tyburn. Once the drink was consumed and the wagon resumed its journey the travellers would be known as "on the wagon", as they would never drink again due to their forthcoming executions.

The pub is now a Fullers brewery owned and operated establishment, having been lovingly restored and re-opened as recently as 2018. Its website describes this as The Swan Hyde Park, bringing the park inside the pub, as it is located directly opposite, with an excellent garden room and drinking area outside immediately facing the park. The pub is also close to Paddington and Kensington Gardens.

The website has an excellent "view gallery" with many carefully produced photos of both the exterior and interior, including of a collection of framed butterflies on one wall. The pub states it has options to suit any size of event, including a birthday party or for somewhere full of character for a London wedding reception and has various elegant dining areas and traditional restaurant style service, with a gastro pub style.

Two Brewers

> **Dates back to at least 1839, steeped in theatrical history and renowned for having a dark and sultry past, featuring open fires and cosy interior following recent refurbishment.**

The pub dates back to at least 1839, where it is referred to in the will of William Filler, Licensed Victualler of the Two Brewers Public House, Little Saint Andrews Street, Seven Dials, Middlesex, which is still held in The National Archives, in Kew, London.

This is also referenced in St Giles pub history, which is a listing of historical public houses, taverns, inns, beer houses and hotels in St Giles in Fields, London. The St Giles in Fields, London listing, uses information from census, trade directories and other historical references to add licensees, bar staff, lodgers and visitors where relevant. Sometime before 1940, the address of the pub was changed from 6 Little St Andrew Street to 40 Monmouth Street, where it has been operating from ever since.

This is situated near the Seven Dials junction in the centre of Covent Garden, in the heart of theatre land. This 18th century traditional styled pub is often referred to as a "theatrical pub" as a result and is popular with actors and film school students. Its history is explained in detail on an attractive plaque by the front entrance, detailing its sinister and chequered past. During the 1600's the area surrounding Monmouth Street was traditionally the home of tradesmen and craftsmen, who sold their wares from small market stalls in the outlying area.

The traders were diverse, from fruit and vegetable merchants to saddlers and horse dealers, the most common being second hand shoe traders, all trying to get by honestly or otherwise. By 1751 the area was changing and became more sinister, renowned for petty crime and murder, the perfect setting for Hogarth's Gin Lanes which was viewed as a mild description of what you might expect to see in Monmouth Street.

Charles Dickens was attracted to the St Giles area, fascinated by its horror and wickedness, basing his novel Bleak House on this part of London, infamous for its slums, crime and numerous accompanying evils.

One attractive feature often overlooked, is a stained glass window in the roof light in the rear part of the bar, which allows some natural light to penetrate. It has a warm and friendly atmosphere, with open fireplaces although is relatively small in comparison to most pubs. Reflecting the links to theatre, there are many old posters, portraits of famous actors and actresses, and other memorabilia taking up most of the limited wall space, relating to historical productions.

The pub is now owned and operated by the Greene King brewery, who completed an extensive refurbishment in July 2019, and it has blossomed into a favourite haunt for theatregoers, having left its dark and sultry past behind. They sell a wide selection of beers and spirits, plus a variety of traditional pub dishes, listed extensively on the pub's website. In addition to this, they also have fruit and quiz machines, which are not often seen in Central London pubs as they take up valuable space, needed for additional standing room. The welcome in this pub is friendly, inviting and memorable, a far cry from its sombre past!

126 Newgate Street, Newgate, EC1A 7AA

Viaduct Tavern

Authentic Victorian former gin palace, near a one time jail, with original cashier's booth and grand wall frescoes, plus extensive use of glass and mirrors throughout.

Work began on the construction of the 1,400 foot long Holborn Viaduct, spanning the valley of the River Fleet and Holborn Hill, in 1863, and was completed in 1869 to be officially opened by Queen Victoria. The Viaduct Tavern was opened in the same year, its name celebrating the remarkable, for the time, feat of engineering, no doubt with the expectation of early patronage from construction workers.

As a surviving late Victorian pub, built in 1874, the design was in line with the ornate gin palaces that arose during the earlier part of the 19th century, with extensive use of glass and mirrors. The interior was re-modelled between 1898 and 1900 by Arthur Dixon, a leading light in the arts and crafts movement. There is the early use of the traditional bar to speed up the serving of gin, often with no seating areas leading to standing only consumption. These palaces continued to be built after the decline of gin drinking and this pub remains an excellent example.

The various entrance doors suggest that this pub was once divided into several snugs or booths around the original bar, which has an ornate arched frontage. The "stillion" or back bar fitting is also made with elegant glass panels with motifs. The high moulded ceilings are covered and bordered with deep red Lincrusta style embossed coves, made from linseed oil gel and wood flour, on a paper base.

The images of women, painted on the large wooden panels on the back walls, are said to represent "Agriculture, Banking and Arts." These are largely still intact, apart from minor damage inflicted by a drunken soldier on leave during the First World War, leaving a small hole, probably a bullet hole, in the roof.

They are signed by the artist, simply as "Hal". The elegantly carved Managers office, at the back of the bar, was originally a booth or cashier's office for the landlord to exchange tokens for various drinks. This was way before tills and ensured the money did not end up in the wrong hands. The tokens were occasionally found elsewhere including on demolition sites. Look out for the carving showing that Opium and Prostitutes were available upstairs.

When the pub first opened, the infamous Newgate Prison still stood across the road, prior to its demolition in 1902. Next to the pub was the Giltspur Street Compter, a debtors' and petty criminals' prison. Ancient foundations have been found in the area and there has been speculation that some of these might have been alongside the prison cells. In the very deep basement of the pub are seven or eight structures that resemble cells, although they are more likely to have been old storage facilities or part of the Compter. The pub staff may allow customers to go down to visit these, whatever their original use, although best to mind the steep steps.

The Newgate gallows also stood on the road right in front of the pub, being the site of London's last public executions, where ghosts are felt to linger around, apparently with the minor prank of turning off the toilet lights. These links have made the pub popular with ghost hunters, where the occasional séance is held, although the ghosts do have weekends off as the pub is closed. Nowadays the pub stands opposite the Old Bailey, where Oscar Wilde once appeared, during his trial. The Viaduct Tavern is now owned and operated by Fullers brewery, and popular with postal workers from the nearby Giltspur depot.

14-16 Rupert Street, Soho, W1D 6DD

Waxy O'Connors

Like no other, with a labyrinth of unique bars on various levels, Irish themed and with an interior with amazing features, including cathedral like timber carvings and remains of a tree from Ireland.

The pub's website suggests you should first check out the background to Waxy O'Connor, born in Smithfield, Dublin City, in 1788. He gained his name as a result of his profession as a candle maker, although had a legendary reputation for his capacity to consume hard liquor. The stated excuse for such indulgences was that candle makers had to work in such extreme heat, that it sapped a man of both energy and fluids. O'Connor commented at one point "Such heat does parch a man, a parched man is a barren man, and beer is the only cure, ah us lads could put away gallons in a day".

Water, it seems, was an unknown elixir and beer was intended to be used for medical purposes to cure un-specified illnesses. Waxy O'Connor's "tree" was planted 250 years ago in the middle of Ireland and died naturally in 1994. A local woodworker, who played around the beech tree as a boy, hewed the pieces that were then shipped to England to be carefully planted in Waxy O'Connor's pub in August 1995. So now a tree, which has lived for a quarter of a millennium in Ireland, has begun an extended lease of life in the heart of Soho, Central London, where the trunk and branches are carefully preserved and on show.

The pub is now regarded as London's biggest and best Irish bar, which is a significant claim indeed. This is in an unassuming looking building at street level, although behind the discreet façade is a labyrinth of 4 quite unique bars over 6 different levels. This really is like no other bar or restaurant you have ever visited. The extraordinary interior has some amazing features including cathedral like carvings in timber, stained glass windows and beautifully tiled floors, across a warren of staircases and passages.

It has gained worldwide recognition for its warm hospitality, where each bar area has its own atmosphere and personality, and there is felt to be something for everyone here. Live music events are hosted four nights a week, including traditional Irish sessions every Sunday night, plus other promotions, which provide a highly lively atmosphere at most times.

This also has three large screens for showing all major sporting events, primarily rugby and football, reflecting the international nature of the clientele. Extending this further, the pub hosts celebrations throughout the year for New Year, Australia Day, National Irish Coffee Day and Halloween. The main celebrations are of course reserved for St Patrick's Day, when the pub becomes a major meeting place for all the Irish in London to experience their unique approach to this key annual event.

The pub serves traditional homemade dishes, plus an extensive range of beers, spirits and whiskeys. You can even hire a private area with your very own bar for birthday, work leaving dos, Christmas parties or other celebrations, where you can take your pick of the various bar areas.

The pub's website has a 360 degree view through a virtual tour, which could take some time to work around, although clearly easier than doing this on the ground. The Irish Hospitality Global Awards proudly presented the pub with the Irish pub of the year - Europe award in 2018, which is prominently displayed on their website.

191 Drury Lane, Covent Garden, WC2B 5QD

White Hart

> **Old Bailey archives reveal this to be the first licenced premises dating back to 1216, notorious as a watering hole for highwaymen, attractive bar area with natural light streaming in through a skylight.**

This is a pub that reputedly dates back to 1216, and Old Bailey archives reveal the corner of Drury Lane and High Holborn, where this is located, as having the oldest licensed premises of London. The "Whyte Hart Public House" has been the name of pubs on this site since the 15th century, which has had, unsurprisingly, a colourful past. This has been known as a legendary watering hole for London's notorious highwayman and other rogues.

In the 16th and 17th centuries, Drury Lane was known as a fashionable street, with residents including the likes of The Marquess of Argyll, Oliver Cromwell and Nell Gwynne. However, the area of Drury Lane became one of the worst slums in London in the 18th century, when it became notable for drunkenness, brawls and prostitution. Legend has it that Richard (Dick) Turpin was a regular, along with other thieves and even came in for a pint prior to his hanging in 1739. Condemned men habitually stopped in for a last drink and whatever comfort could be offered by women, before facing the hangman's noose.

The White Hart is described as the first addition of the Morton Scott Pub Company, when they took ownership of this beautiful and charming pub in 2003. As a company, they are passionate about keeping the spirit of London pubs alive. This now forms the key part of their family of three public houses, conveniently near Holborn station, and in the Covent Garden area, including the Sun Tavern in Long Acre and the Marquis in Chandos Place. As these are all within walking distance of each other they could easily make a great pub crawl adventure, where the operators encourage you to visit the rest of the family.

The outside has a sign encouraging customers to eat drink and relax, particularly extolling the virtues of their good, honest food, which is what they provide, if that's what floats your boat, for under a ten pound note, with homemade meals, prepared daily and using fresh produce, all under £10. The last time we were in we got involved briefly in a delivery where local suppliers are clearly well known and welcomed as part of the family operating this pub. There is a raised dining area towards the rear of the pub, which is well lit, with plenty of natural light streaming in.

Just inside the entrance, there are four comfortable, black leather chairs, ideal for sitting in the window, to read the paper, and watch people walking past on Drury Lane. Look out for the two pictures of birds alongside and two figures guarding the entrance door on the inside, surrounded by various pewter tankards. There are also many beautifully engraved mirrors alongside pictures, with mostly floral scenes, on the white panelled walls.

The owners hope you enjoy the vibrant atmosphere this historic pub has to offer, hosting monthly drink specials to "sweeten the libations", and to encourage the temptation to stay for one more drink. They have a big screen TV showing Sky Sports which, when not on, appears to have a relaxing backing scene of tropical fish swimming seemingly without a care in the world, which seems to exemplify the attitude encouraged for spending time in this historic establishment.

1 Groveland Court, Cheapside, EC4M 9EH

Williamson's Tavern

> Unique and hidden away, originally the residence of the Lord Mayor, then converted back from a hotel, holding the oldest excise licence in The City, with a ghostly poltergeist.

Williamson's Tavern has a plaque outside stating that it dates back to the 17th century and built not long after the Great Fire of London of 1666. This is located off Cheapside, along Bow Lane, amongst back lanes and small alleys in which Charles Dickens based much of A Christmas Carol and various scenes from The Pickwick Papers. The pub is located halfway down Bow Lane, in Groveland Court, some two minutes' stroll from Mansion House station, although you will need to be fortunate to stumble upon this if you are not clear where you are going.

The pub is said to hold the oldest excise license in the City and was originally built as a private residence. The site became the address of the new Lord Mayor of London and its wrought iron gates were gifts from William III and Mary II, who were said to have dined here.

By 1739 the building was not thought to be grand enough, for an address of the Lord Mayor and it was sold to Robert Williamson for conversion into a hostel, although the Lord Mayor remained until 1752, when he finally moved to Mansion House. The hotel became a mid-priced favourite for merchants and sea-farers on leave and remained in the Williamson family until 1914, when James Williamson died. It was then sold at auction and became the grand old tavern that we know today, although most of the present building dates from an extensive rebuild in 1932, reflecting the style of the pre-war period.

A myth exists that Williamson's marks the exact centre of the City, this is unproven, although it definitely stands on ancient foundations. Roman bricks were discovered during renovation works in 1939, which are featured in the front bar fireplace. One legacy is that a lucky few may even bear witness to the ghost of Martha, a poltergeist whose very presence has led to police dogs growling as they pass the end of the lane and they often flatly refuse to come any closer. The pub's website refers to the fact that there is no painting to be found of Martha in the building at all, which is described as a curiosity. Some longer serving members of staff do, however, recall seeing the same dark painting in different parts of the pub. There is a sign outside for Martha's dining room though, even poltergeists have to eat.

Like other pubs operated by the Nicholson's chain, which are known for their individual style, exciting stories and charming personalities, the pub offers cards for sale as the perfect gift for the food and drink lover. These gifts will no doubt encourage recipients to pop in for a pint of well-kept cask ale, other drinks or a hearty bit to eat.

One particularly impressive offering is to join regulars and tourists every Wednesday evening from 7 pm, when you can listen to unique stories, on a relaxed walking tour through the winding streets of Central London. This allows you to learn about the astounding heritage of this and other Nicholson's pubs, experienced over 2 hours or so with your guide, prior to sitting down for dinner at their speciality sausage and chop house The Walrus and Carpenter. This tour is recommended for adults only and remains very popular.

145 Fleet Street, Blackfriars, EC4A 2BU

Ye Olde Cheshire Cheese

World renowned with extensive history, various bars on several levels, wood panelled and truly "olde", with illustrious former clientele of literary figures primarily Dr Samuel Johnson.

This pub was severely damaged in the great Fire of 1666, having already been established for some 100 years, although re-opened a year later, adopting the name Ye Olde Cheshire Cheese. The pub is located down Wine Office Court, just off Fleet Street and has changed very little, with its white-washed stone walls, low oak beams, dark wood panels and tall backed benches from its 17th century origins. The age is celebrated with a plaque by the front door, listing the fifteen monarchs who have reigned whilst the pub has been operating.

Fleet Street became the home of the British press, when a small printing shop in Shoe Lane was established in 1500, supplying the legal trade with printing as this became available. The great writers of the day moved into the area and the pub became particularly associated with Dr Samuel Johnson, who lived close by at 17 Gough Square, and was known to equally enjoy an ale, tobacco and food. Dr Johnson is recognised, with his own corner dedicated to him, including, apparently, his favourite chair and a copy of his famous dictionary.

It was known that the pub stood on the sacred ground of a Carmelite Monastery since the 1300's. Remarkably, a further fire occurred in 1962 on the upper storey, which unveiled some clues to its history, as various pornographic tiles became visible from its time as some form of gentlemen's club in the 18th century, or maybe even a brothel upstairs. The tiles have been removed and are on show at the Museum of London rather than being left for visitors to the pub to see. Inns were often allowed to become mixed use, as unofficial employment exchanges, courtrooms and other uses in the 18th and 19th centuries.

A chair dedicated to Charles Dickens is on show, as another earlier regular, plus a parrot in a cage. This is not however the famous Polly, an African Grey, who squawked famously in the pub and mimicked its customers for some 40 years, even learning to swear in various languages and imitate the sound of champagne corks popping. These performances led to Polly getting her own obituary in some 200 publications in the international press in 1926.

The interior has a chophouse on the ground floor, which was one of the earliest steakhouses in London and still in use today. The meat was chopped and cooked on a gridiron over an open fire and served on the plate without any particular accompaniments. This simple style of cooking became popular and developed through the 19th century, when you would be served with jacket potatoes and the eponymous Cheshire cheese, which you could ask to be served hot and bubbling in a small pan.

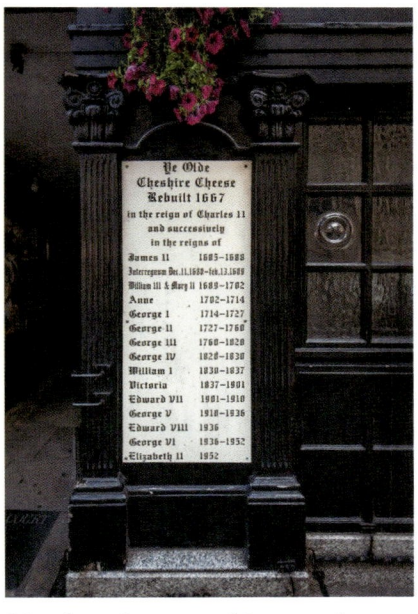

The pub attracts many tourists, especially at the weekends, to experience what attracted many literary figures to visit over the years. In addition to Dickens and Dr Johnson, Mark Twain, Sir Arthur Conan Doyle, Alfred Lord Tennyson and P.G. Wodehouse were also regulars, when it had become something of a gentlemen's club, with long serving waiters, one even having a painting of him still displayed.

There is also an old and very small spit and sawdust bar, a maze of ancient rooms connected by dark passageways and very low ceilings. A sign over one bar states that gentlemen only will be served, this is fortunately not a practise still observed. A sense of claustrophobia is however helped by the various warming fireplaces. The pub rightly retains its status on the Campaign for Real Ale's National Inventory of Historic Pub Interiors.

Ye Olde Cock Tavern

> Dating originally from 1549 and on its present site since 1887, very narrow frontage although with extensive long interior bar areas, which have hosted Pepys, Dickens and Dr Johnson amongst others.

Located at the western end of Fleet Street, it claims to have the narrowest pub frontage in London, described as one that if you blink, you will miss it. This dates from 1887 in its present location, and is extremely tall by comparison, over 5 floors, timber framed, and now Grade 2 listed.

There is an elegant carved wooden cock and a ground floor frontage that some have attributed to the renowned wood carver, Grinling Gibbons, which means it would have been moved from the previous building. This was originally named The Cock and Bottle standing on the opposite side of Fleet Street from the 17th century, and parts of it miraculously survived the Great Fire of 1666.

This was a regular haunt of Samuel Pepys, who wrote in his diary of an assignation here with a Mrs Knipps, one of his many lady friends. Many other great literary figures have drunk here, including Charles Dickens, Lord Alfred Tennyson, William Makepeace Thackeray, Oliver Goldsmith and inevitably Dr Samuel Johnson.

Lord Tennyson, who was Poet Laureate from 1850 until his death on 1892, who was the most impactful as his "Will Waterproof's Lyrical Monologue" started "O plump head waiter at The Cock, To which I most resort, how goes the time? Tis five o'clock, go fetch a pint of port".

The original tavern was demolished in 1886, when the Bank of England built a large branch to serve customers in the adjacent law courts, although The Cock was re-built on the opposite side of the street, likely again to be assisted by the work of the wood carver, Grinling Gibbons.

Given the exterior appearance, it is no surprise that the interior has a long, narrow, ground floor bar stretching some way back from the street, with an original flagstone floor. This has been worn smooth over many years, with a traditional environment. There are a succession of small areas with ceilings of various heights, dark wooden panelling, some bare brick, and all with old photos throughout. The side bar has fancy hundi lights above and dark carved wood under the counter. There is a small mezzanine area at the back supported by thick wooden beams, and a snug underneath.

Many of the original ornaments were unfortunately destroyed by fire in 1990, although an oak fireplace believed to be some 400 years old survived and remains in the first floor bar. This area allows you to look out over Fleet Street, whilst admiring portraits of many of the famous former customers, who remain an iconic part of its history.

The pub is now owned and operated by Greene King, one of the country's leading retailers and brewers, running over 3,100 pubs, restaurants and hotels across England, Scotland and Wales. The pub has a fantastic feature on its website, where you can take a video guided tour of the pub, across all 3 floors that they operate from, and has a "get social" section so you can keep up to date with everything that is going on there.

The pub has been introducing a selection of delicious gins, to encourage customers to head down to ensure they don't miss the gin of the moment! They are so confident that they have a G&T guarantee to provide the perfect gin and tonic, or they will replace it for free. They also have an extensive beer and food selection. The TV appears to be always on, showing sports and news on a continuous feed which most customers like although some don't, very much due to personal taste of course.

Ye Olde Mitre

> Traditional 1546 pub, hard to find, tucked way down a small alleyway, with close links to royalty and key figures from the Elizabethan era, with various framed historical pictures.

Often thought of as the most difficult London pub to find, as it is tucked away down an alley off Hatton Garden. After heavy duty shopping in all the jewellery shops in this world-famous area for diamonds, the pub offers some welcome refreshment. Even people who work nearby don't know of its existence, which is not surprising given the deliberate lack of clear signage and directions.

A sign above the pub, however, states that it was built in 1546 although it is more likely that the majority of it was constructed around 1772, as a faithful depiction of the original Elizabethan alehouse. The stone mitre built in the exterior wall was rescued from the Palace of Ely, that used to stand nearby, although the only remaining evidence of this is Ely Chapel. This dates back to 1280 and is the oldest Catholic Church in England.

The Palace of Ely hosted King Henry VIII and his first wife, Catherine of Aragon, for several days in 1531. This was before the pub was built, although subsequently The Mitre Tavern was created as an alternative refuge for the servants, who worked at the palace, although still very close by and remained under the control of the church. Shakespeare talks about the Palace in Richard III, when the Duke of Gloucester refers to being lost around Holborn.

Royal links were continued as Elizabeth I and a gentleman friend, Sir Christopher Hatton, were once spotted dancing around a cherry tree, that stood in front of the original Mitre, using this as a maypole. Hatton became a successful Lord Chancellor and commandeered the land, through the payment of a rent to the Bishop of one red rose a year. The cherry tree can still be seen, as the pub was built around it in 1772, visible behind a glass panel in the corner of the bar. Technically the Mitre and Ely Palace are still in Cambridgeshire, where the Metropolitan police in theory have no power to impose the law.

The entrance to the pub is through an elegant wooden door, with several barrels positioned in the small courtyard outside, to be used as tables for drinks. There is a small but attractive blue plaque on the side wall, stating that by virtue of the historic interest, this pub merits the title of "Taylor Walker, Heritage Site".

Inside, the pub is relatively small with plenty of wood and brewery-related objects dotted around the walls. There is a much larger seating area in another room with its own bar and a snug room off to one side, named Ye Closet. More pub artefacts adorn the walls with a collection of empty beer bottles high up on various shelves. Up a few stairs is The Bishop's Room, which is used by customers to escape the crowded main bar, and gives some clue as to the pub's origins. This area can be hired for private events. It is possible to peer in to the windows of jewellers' workshops back on Hatton Garden and witness repairs in progress, whilst enjoying this now Fullers brewery operated pub.

The lack of space precludes the provision of an extensive food menu, beyond toasted sandwiches although it does have a reputation for how many good quality sandwiches can be churned out.

29 Watling Street, Mansion House, EC4M 9BR

Ye Olde Watling

Pub with a long history, famous for providing an office for Sir Christopher Wren, whilst he was working on the construction of St Paul's Cathedral straight after the Great Fire of 1666.

Watling Street is an old Roman road that ran the breadth of the country from Dover, via London, over to Wales, establishing London as a key staging post on the way. As you walk up Watling Street, a couple of minutes off Cheapside, you come to the pub with a magnificent view down to St Paul's Cathedral. The pub was built by Sir Christopher Wren in 1668 in the immediate aftermath of the Great Fire, although still has a reasonable claim for being the oldest surviving tavern in London. This was constructed largely from old ships' timbers.

Wren used an upstairs office as his drawing room, whilst working on plans for and the subsequent construction of the cathedral, quite a claim to fame! There are uninterrupted views of the great Cathedral from outside the pub. It is believed that many of his workmen also stayed in the pub, whilst working on the construction project, as this is only a very short walk away, and also gave them somewhere to drink and no doubt the opportunity for Wren to keep an eye on them as construction progressed. Other iconic attractions are also close by including the Millennium Bridge and The Royal Exchange, within the City of London.

Now owned by Nicholson's, who are renowned for operating pubs with individual style, exciting stories and charming personalities. This is one of the rare gems in their collection of iconic and great pubs, held in the highest regard, although little of what we now see can reliably be said to date back to 1666. The building underwent a major renovation in 1901 and was well regarded for its luncheons in Edwardian times. It was referred to in E. Montizambert's "Unnoticed London" as the "Old Watling Restaurant" in 1922. A surviving etched glass panel on the door that opens out on to Bow Lane, still refers to this as a "dining room".

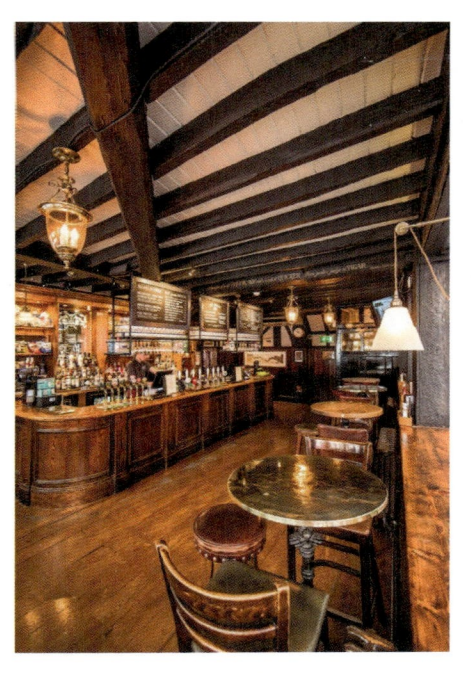

The interior has been restored since the Blitz, with extensive wood panelling and a decorative bar with a collection of prints from Sir Christopher Wren on the walls, depicting his various works. The main ground floor bar is typical of a City pub, with little seating, although the rear part is quiet and calm, with tables to sit at arranged in a restaurant style. There are sturdy wooden beams above and even a portrait of Sir Christopher Wren looking down from one wall. The front entrance to St Mary Aldermary can be seen through the large windows, which was also built by Wren.

The pub's website refers to this as being a great spot to catch up with friends, chat with colleagues, and generally enjoy the finer things in life in unique surroundings. Their menu is summarised as serving seasonal specialities and mouth-watering favourites. This has a "news and offers" section and has been creating good news for hundreds of years. One particularly attractive offer was for runners in the London Marathon, to show their medal upon completion and get their first drink free, probably the most well deserved that they will ever receive. You can even sign up to receive the pub's regular newsletters so the news can be sent directly to you, including relating to forthcoming major sporting events being shown.

Honourable Mentions

We have prepared these to include a few pubs that deserve a mention, although they just missed the cut of *The 50 Greatest Pubs in Central London*. This includes where they are located close to, but just the wrong side of the defined catchment area of the London underground Circle line.

Readers will be able to see that the "maps" applications on mobile phones clearly shows the precise route of all underground lines, so referencing this makes it clear and unambiguous if a pub is located inside or outside our defined catchment area.

29 Greek Street, Soho, W1D 5DH
London Underground: Leicester Square (Northern and Piccadilly Lines)

Coach & Horses

This may have been the last pub in Soho with a celebrity landlord, back when it was a local neighbourhood pub, who is still fondly remembered today. Norman "You're barred" Balon was known for quick quips and lack of patience. Customers flocked to the pub for a dressing down and to experience Norman's unique approach to hospitality, where he presided for some 60 years.

An attractive, although largely unremarkable pub, established in 1847, customers now tend to congregate outside on the pavement and this remains a favourite of journalists. The staff of Private Eye, the satirical publication, frequently lunched in the pub which was chronicled by the famous bohemian Jeffrey Bernard in his weekly Spectator column during the 1970's. Other customers known to frequent the pub were John Hurt, Peter Cook and Lucian Freud plus other lesser known celebrities, to witness Balon's strict and unique approach to hospitality.

More recently a clean-up has taken place, in keeping with the changes in the area and customers' tastes. This remains a Soho institution although, despite much local opposition, the long standing tenant's lease is not being renewed. This still deserves a visit and mention due to the history and notoriety, largely due to its long-standing ex landlord's unique approach.

47 Aldgate High St, Aldgate, EC3N 1AL
London Underground: Aldgate (Circle and Metropolitan Lines)

Hoop & Grapes

This pub survived the Great Fire of London in September 1666, whilst known as The Castle, due to being located just outside the City walls. The Great Fire destroyed over eighty per cent of all properties within the City walls having raged for four days before finally being extinguished. The pub stands on Aldgate, which was one of the original gates of the City of London, where the original gatehouse was fortified and surrounded by inns to accommodate travellers.

Records show that the building that is now The Hoop and Grapes was constructed in 1592, although the cellars below probably date further back to the 13th century, leaving it with the claim of being one of the oldest pubs in London. As the Great Fire destroyed many of the timber-framed properties, the pub is now a rare example of a medieval building in Central London. The pub's name was changed to The Angel and Crown then traded as a wine merchant called Christopher Hills until becoming The Hoop and Grapes in 1920.

From the outside it appears to be leaning to the East and about to collapse, although was re-enforced with a steel frame in 1983, through a refurbishment preserving the original features. This includes sash windows and two 17th century carved posts, decorated with images of vines, on either side of the front door.

The interior still shows the original layout, although extends beyond the very narrow frontage, with an ingenious communication system between the bar and the very old cellars, for calling down to the cellar man to re-stock the bar. A remarkable and well restored pub, one of the oldest in London, although some 200 metres outside our catchment area, given its location close to Aldgate tube station but being just the wrong side of the Circle Line.

7 Portobello Road, Notting Hill, W11 3DA
London Underground: Notting Hill Gate (Central, Circle and District Lines)

Sun in Splendour

This pub is a particular favourite of the Thirsty crew, and illustrates the approach to the defined catchment area well. It is described by TripAdvisor as a Victorian pub with wooden benches, a snug, whitewashed beer garden and a British comfort food menu. It has an excellent location with a very attractive "Portobello Road W11" street sign on the building directly opposite, providing excellent photo opportunities. Miss Thirsty, on one visit, was inspired and left her refreshments behind for a few moments to pop out to take a photo to share with her friends on social media. Many tourists do similar things risking London traffic, to cross the zebra crossing on Abbey Road, which is famous due to having featured on a Beatles' album cover.

Mrs Thirsty was also, on one other occasion, looking forward to a refreshing gin and tonic after a hard days shopping and sightseeing. She thought it would be appropriate to ask for a Portobello Road gin, as the pub is located on this road, only to be met with a bemused response from the bar staff stating that they had never heard of it. Fortunately, various equally palatable alternatives were available instead.

Despite all the positive features and being close to Notting Hill Gate station, which is the most westerly point on the long established main part of the Circle line, this is slightly on the wrong side of this for direct inclusion in this book.

Index

Abbey Road, 108
Abbot of Westminster, 38
Adelphi Theatre, 54
Alastair Greig, 34
Albert Finney, 82
Aldgate, 107
Alfred Lord Tennyson, 97
American, 34
Andrew Ho, 75
Angel and Crown, 107
Ann Boleyn, 38
Apothecaries Hall, 16
Art Nouveau, 6
Arthur Blomfield, 56
Arthur Conan Doyle, 76, 97
Arthur Dixon, 88
Augustus John, 26
Baker Brothers, 66
Banister Fletcher, 43
Bank of England, 56
Barnabas Blessed, 54
Bartholomew Fair, 36
Baynard Castle, 16
Beatles, 21, 108
Ben Caunt's Head, 74
Berta Schmitt, 30
Blackfriars Monastery, 16
Blackfriars Playhouse, 16
Bristol Shipping Company, 81
British Museum, 62
Bruce Reynolds, 82
Bucket of Blood, 45
Buckingham Palace, 79
Bugell, 10
Bull and Mouth, 50
Bull Inn, 54

Bummarees, 40
Bunce, 52
Bush, 50
Buster Edwards, 82
Cabinet Room, 71
CAMRA, 15, 27, 64, 73, 75, 97
Carmelite Monastery, 96
Cask Marque, 37, 60
Castle, 107
Catherine of Aragon, 100
Cedric, ghost, 32
Charge of the Light Brigade, 50
Charles Allchild, 26
Charles Barry, 70
Charles de Gaulle, 30
Charles Dickens, 10, 37, 42, 70, 86, 94, 96, 98
Charles Hall, 78
Charles V, 7
Charlton Heston, 35
Chelsea Flower Show, 12
Chelsea Pottery, 53
Christmas trees, 12
Christopher Hatton, 100
Christopher Wren, 58, 102
Claude Duval, 84
Clement Atlee, 70
Cloth Fair, 36
Cloudesley Shovell, 78
Coach and Horses, 74
Cock and Bottle, 98
Coopers Arms, 44
Court of Piepowder, 36
Crimea War, 50
Cromwell Bar, 62
Crown and Sugar Loaf, 59, 66

Daniel Edwards, 42
David Hasselhoff, 11
Dennis Nilsen, 75
Devonshire House, 34
Diana Dors, 82
Dick Turpin, 92
Dirk Bogarde, 74
Doctor of Mirth, 60
Doctor William Butler, 60
Don Bradman, 21
Downing Street, 70
Dr Samuel Johnson, 96, 98
Dr Watson, 76
Dr Willis, 68
Drury Lane, 92
Duke of Argyll, 4
Duke of Devonshire, 34
Duke of Gloucester, 100
Duke of Marlborough, 12
Duke of Wellington, 32
Dylan Thomas, 14, 27, 31
E. Montizambert, 102
E.J. Rose, 43
Earl of Bedford, 44
Earl of Dorset, 38
Earl of Rochester, 44
Earl of Salisbury, 74
East India Company, 24
Edward Woodhouse, 79
Edwardian, 84
Elizabeth Taylor, 35
Elizabethan, 50, 100
Elvis Presley, 21
Ely Chapel, 100
Fellowship of Porters, 81
First Royal Regiment of Foot Guards, 32
Fleet Marriages, 38
Flora Murray, 20
Fortnum and Mason, 72
Foundling Hospital, 68
Fountain, 50

Frank Sinatra, 35
Frederick Walton, 5
French, 30
Full Monty, 40
Gaston Berlemont, 31
Geoffrey Chaucer, 70
George Burke, 71
George Carpenter, 30
George Cook, 44
George Orwell, 26
Georgian, 16, 72
German Restaurant, 60
Gerry O'Brien, 12
Gibbet at Tyburn, 84
Giltspur Street Compter, 89
Grand Dame of Queer Street, 18
Great Fire, 10, 16, 46, 49, 50, 58, 60, 94, 98, 102, 107
Great Ormond Street Hospital, 68
Great Train Robbery, 82
Grenadier Guards, 32
Grinling Gibbons, 98
Grosvenor Estate, 23
Harold Wilson, 13
Harrods, 66
Harry Potter, 47
Hatton Garden, 100
Haunch of Venison, 56
Henekey's bar, 14
Henley and Sons, 63
Henry Ireton, 62
Her Majesty's Treasury, 71
Holborn Viaduct, 88
Hoop and Grapes, 107
Hopping House, 70
Horace Jones, 46
Horn Alehouse, 10
Horn Coffee House, 10
Horn Tavern, 10
Houses of Parliament, 70
Inigo Jones, 44
Ireland, 90

Irish Hospitality Global Awards, 91
Isambard Kingdom Brunel, 71
J. Tyler & Sons, 65
Jack Dempsey, 30
Jack Nicklaus, 35
James Mason, 53
James Pardy, 46
James Williamson, 94
Jampot, 42
Jeffrey Bernard, 106
John Bradshaw, 62
John Dryden, 44
John Hurt, 106
John Lennon, 21
John Mortimer, 31
John Soane, 70
John Spencer-Churchill, 12
John Thomas Wimpers, 23
Judah "Pop" Kleinfield, 26
Kenneth Williams, 26
Kevin Moran, 52
King and Keys, 48
King Charles II, 51, 54, 62
King George III, 26, 68
King Henry VIII, 6, 7, 8, 38, 44, 80, 100
King James I, 60
King Richard III, 100
King William III, 94
Kings Arms, 8
Kray twins, 54
Lamplighter, 9
Laurel and Hardy, 63
Law Courts, 56
Leadenhall Market, 46
Lesley Lewis, 31
Lewis Henry Isaacs, 40
Liberace, 19
Lincoln's Inn Fields, 80
Lincrusta style, 5, 88
Lloyds's Avenue Conservation Area, 24

Lord Aberconway, 48
Lord Alfred Tennyson, 98
Lord Berkeley, 34
Lord Mayor of London, 36, 94
Louisa Garrett Anderson, 20
Lucian Freud, 106
Maggie Smith, 74
Magpie Ale House, 24
Mansion House, 94
Mark Twain, 97
Marquess of Argyll, 92
Marquis, 92
Marquis of Salisbury, 74
Martha, poltergeist, 94
Marylebone Cricket Club, 9
Mason's Company, 60
Masonic Lodge, 80
Matthew Allam, 68
Maurice Chevalier, 30
Merchant Taylor's Company, 36
Michael Bentine, 27
Millennium Bridge, 11, 102
Mohammed Al Fayed, 66
Mourning Bush, 50
Mrs Lovett, 57
Napoleon, 32
Nathaniel Curzon, 68
Nell Gwynne, 92
Netherlands, 52
Newgate Prison, 89
Nina Hammett, 26
Noel Coward Theatre, 75
Norman Balon, 106
Northumberland Arms, 76
Nottinghamshire Giant, 74
Old Bailey, 89, 92
Old English Divan, 60
Old Tom's Bar, 47
Oliver Cromwell, 62, 92
Oliver Goldsmith, 98
Only Running Footman, 28
Oscar Wilde, 74, 89

P.G. Wodehouse, 97
Pac-Man's Drinking Den, 48
Paddy Kennedy, 83
Palace of Westminster, 71
Palace Theatre, 8
Pasqual Rosee's Head, 42
Pasque Rosee, 42
Patmac's Railway Buffet, 48
Pear Shaped Comedy Club, 27
Peter Cook, 106
Peter O'Toole, 82
Philip Seymour Hoffman, 74
Physic Gardens, 84
Pierce Brosnan, 55
Polly, parrot, 96
Portobello Road, 108
Pound, 34
Prince Albert, 64
Prince Charles, 47
Princess Louise, 64
Princess Margaret, 35
Private Eye, 106
PUB LOCATION
    Bayswater, 84
    Belgravia, 32, 52, 82
    Bloomsbury, 68
    City of London, 6, 10, 16, 24, 36, 38, 40, 42, 46, 48, 50, 56, 58, 60, 66, 88, 94, 96, 98, 100, 102, 107, 108
    Covent Garden, 20, 44, 86, 92
    Fitzrovia, 28
    Holborn, 14, 62, 64, 80
    Mayfair, 26, 34, 72
    Notting Hill, 12
    Piccadilly, 22
    Soho, 4, 8, 18, 30, 74, 90, 106
    Strand, 54
    Westminster, 70, 76, 78
PUB OPERATOR
    City Pub Company, 54
    Ei Group, 40

Fuller's, 12, 44, 70, 72, 82, 84, 88, 100
Greene King, 26, 50, 62, 74, 76, 86, 98
Hall & Woodhouse, 78
Independent, 10, 16, 20, 30, 36, 52, 68, 80, 90, 106
McMullen & Sons, 56
Metropolitan, 32
Mitchell & Butler Group, 108
Morton Scott Pub Company, 92
Nicholson's, 4, 6, 8, 48, 58, 94, 102, 107
Samuel Smith's, 14, 22, 28, 64, 96
Shepherd Neame, 24, 38, 42, 60
Stonegate Pubs, 18
Urban Pubs & Bars, 66
Young's, 34, 46
PUBS FEATURED
    Black Friar, 6
    Centre Page, 10
    Churchill Arms, 12
    Cittie of Yorke, 14
    Coach and Horses, 106
    Cockpit, 16
    Comptons, 18
    Cross Keys, 20
    Duke of Argyll, 22
    East India Arms, 24
    Fitzroy Tavern, 26
    French House, 30
    Hand & Shears, 36
    Hoop & Grapes, 107
    Hoop & Grapes (Farringdon), 38
    Jamaica Wine House, 42
    Lamb & Flag, 44
    Lamb Tavern, 46
    Lord Aberconway, 48
    Lord Raglan, 50
    Nags Head, 52
    Nell Gwynne, 54
    Old Bank of England, 56

Old Bell, 58
Old Doctor Butlers Head, 60
Old Red Lion, 62
Princess Louise, 64
Punch Tavern, 66
Queen's Larder, 68
Red Lion, 72
Red Lion (Westminster), 70
Sherlock Holmes, 76
Ship & Shovell, 78
Ship Tavern, 80
Star Tavern, 82
Sun in Splendour, 108
The Argyll, 4
The Cambridge, 8
The Footman, 28
The Grenadier, 32
The Guinea Grill, 34
The Hope, 40
The Salisbury, 74
The Swan, 84
Two Brewers, 86
Viaduct Tavern, 88
Waxy O'Connors, 90
White Hart, 92
Williamson's Tavern, 94
Ye Olde Cheshire Cheese, 96
Ye Olde Cock Tavern, 98
Ye Olde Mitre, 100
Ye Olde Watling, 102
Punch & Judy, 66
Punch Magazine, 66
Queen Anne, 68
Queen Charlotte, 26, 68
Queen Elizabeth I, 80, 100
Queen Mary II, 94
Queen Mother, 47
Queen Victoria, 64, 88
R. Morris Ltd., 65
R.L. Stevenso, 68
Raglan Hotel, 50
Raoul De Vere, 70

Red Lyon, 62
Refreshment Room, 48
Richard Burton, 35
Richardsons, 54
Robert Cecil, 74
Robert Sawyer, 4
Robert Walpole, 13
Robert Williamson, 94
Roman, 46, 50, 94
Roundheads, 62
Royal Army Medical Corps, 21
Royal English House, 8
Running Horse, 28
Salisbury Stores, 74
Sally Fiber, 27
Samuel Butler, 44
Samuel Johnson, 96, 98
Samuel Pepys, 10, 42, 54, 98
Saracen's Head, 84
Saville and Martin, 66
Seven Dials, 86
Shakespeare, 16
Sherlock Holmes, 76
Sir John Betjeman, 6
Sir Winston Churchill, 12
Smithfield, 40
Sophia Loren, 82
South Coast Raiders, 82
Spectator, 106
St Bartholomew's Hospital, 37
St Bride's Church, 58
St Giles and St George Workhouse, 20
St Giles in Fields, 86
St Giles-in-the-Field, 20
St Mary Aldermary, 103
St Paul's Cathedral, 10, 102
Stephen Sondheim, 58
Sun Tavern, 92
Sweeney Todd, 56, 58
Swiss Hotel, 18
Swiss Tavern, 18

Sylvia Syms, 74
Taylor Walker, Heritage Site, 101
The Bishop's Room, 101
The Hundred Marks, 26
The Royal Exchange, 102
Thomas Constable, 44
Thomas Crapper, 83
Thomas Gresham, 46
Thomas Sackville, 38
Three Castles, 16
Three Mills, 9
Todd's, 43
Tommy Cooper, 26
Tower of London, 24
Turks Head, 42
UNDERGROUND STATIONS
   Aldgate, 24, 107
   Bank, 42, 46, 60
   Barbican, 36
   Blackfriars, 6, 16, 38, 58, 66, 96
   Chancery Lane, 14
   Covent Garden, 20, 54
   Embankment, 76, 78
   Farringdon, 40, 48, 92, 100
   Goodge Street, 28
   Green Park, 26, 34, 72
   Holborn, 62, 64, 80
   Hyde Park Corner, 32
   Knightsbridge, 52, 82
   Lancaster Gate, 84
   Leicester Square, 8, 18, 30, 44, 74, 86, 90, 106

Mansion House, 94, 102
Notting Hill Gate, 12, 108
Oxford Circus, 4
Piccadilly Circus, 22
Russell Square, 68
St Paul's, 10, 50, 88
Temple, 56, 98
Westminster, 70
Union Jack, 28
Victor Berlemont, 30
Victorian, 14, 22, 24, 26, 29, 36, 48, 50, 56, 60, 62, 64, 66, 71, 74, 76, 108
W.A. Williams and Hopton, 18
Walrus and Carpenter, 95
Walter Gibb and Sons, 72
Westminster, 70
Westminster Abbey, 44
Whyte Hart, 92
William Butler, 60
William Filler, 86
William Hogarth, 86
William Kent, 70
William Makepeace Thackeray, 98
William Nicholson, 8
William Terris, 54
Winston Churchill, 70
Ye Closet, 101
Ye Olde Bell Tavern, 58
Ye Olde Cock Tavern, 56
York Minster, 30

Author's Acknowledgements

I would like to acknowledge the generous support and help from the rest of the Thirsty crew in my efforts to produce this book, over a year or so.

Specific thanks to Gordon, Hilda, Jan and Clare Hirst, respectively my Dad, Wife, Sister and Daughter, who provided lots of loving encouragement and helpful suggestions along the way. This has been supplemented by equally key contributions from Dan Forster, Jon Green and Stephen McDowell in their own areas of expertise or knowledge, truly a team effort in creating the content.

Finally to gratefully acknowledge the valuable contribution of Mike Feather for all photography, whose extensive other work can be viewed at www.mikefeather.com.

Thanks also to the Queens Larder where it all started.

NOTES

NOTES

NOTES

NOTES

Available worldwide from Amazon

http://getbook.at/GPLON

———————

http://mtp.agency

http://facebook.com/mtp.agency

@mtp_agency

Printed in Great Britain
by Amazon